ARMED RESPONSE

*A Comprehensive Guide to Using
Firearms for Self-Defense*

By
David S. Kenik

Foreword By
Massad Ayoob

*Brad
Shoot till
the threat
Stops*

Armed Response ®

Published by
ASD Publishing

ISBN 0-9762806-0-4

Manufactured in the United States of America

DEDICATION

I dedicate this book to my wife, Jill, and son, Jared, who are the reasons that I carry. When together, I carry to protect them. When alone, I carry so I may return to them.

TABLE OF CONTENTS

ACKNOWLEDGEMENTS

This book was written for those of us who have taken upon themselves the ultimate responsibility, the protection of the ones we love. I wrote it to inform and inspire in the hopes that the good guys remain safe.

A special thanks goes to Ralph Mroz, who encouraged and assisted me in my efforts, both to expand my understanding and to share the knowledge that I have attained.

Many thanks to Jeff Jennings, whose sharp eyes, and editing skills helped make this book readable.

Don Selesky also deserves well-earned thanks for his efforts to preview the book and assist in editing. His contribution has helped me to better interpret my thoughts and this book is the better for it.

In addition to Ralph and Don, my wife Jill, and Jim Archer also graciously posed for photographs for the book. Thanks to all.

ABOUT THE AUTHOR

Receiving his first 'permit to carry' at the age of 18, David Kenik has been an avid shooter for over twenty years. He is a certified NRA instructor and a regular competitor in IDPA and IPSC matches. His interests include not only handguns, but shotguns and rifles as well.

David learned the shooting craft the hard way...practice and testing. Reading gun magazine after gun magazine, experience taught him not everything that is printed is true. That hard won realization was the catalyst for the writing of this book.

His 'professional' training began with his first of several courses at Lethal Force Institute and continued with instruction from other internationally recognized use of force programs in the judicious use of lethal force, firearms, defensive shooting, weapon disarming and retention, edged weapons, and defensive sprays.

As a gun rights advocate, David co-founded and is a Past Chairman of Citizens' Rights Action League, a state-wide group that advocated the right to self-defense and lobbied against gun control legislation in Rhode Island. Under his leadership CRAL was, and continues to be, an effective force against restrictions upon law-abiding citizens.

David Kenik is the co-founder and Executive Director of the Police Officers Safety Association, Inc, a non-profit organization that offers enhanced training to law enforcement officers.

FOREWORD
By Massad Ayoob

I've known David Kenik for several years. He's a fast man with a pistol and a good shot, but much more important, he has a logical and practical turn of mind.

You see, this armed self-defense business is a whole lot more about the software than the hardware. Dave knows this, and that's why the book you're holding spends a lot more time talking about attitude, mind-set, and self-knowledge than it does about revolver versus autoloading pistol or 9mm versus .45. As Steinbeck wrote, "The mind is the weapon. All else is supplemental." It's your brain that will lead you to prevail in a violent encounter. The firearm is just one of your tools.

Some who look at this book may think its author is giving cops a bad rap. Having worn the badge of a sworn law enforcement officer and supervisor for thirty years, I can tell you he's being frank. What Kenik is telling you is simply that in the United States, law enforcement is necessarily reactive rather than proactive. As much as we try to prevent crime, we generally have to wait until someone calls us before we can act. There are fewer than a million cops in this nation of almost 250 million citizens. Moreover, this is not a country that wants a cop on every doorstop. That would be the KGB, not the model of policing that American citizens have made clear that they want.

Thus, the cop stands in much the same position with the potential crime victim as the trauma surgeon does with the potential accident victim. Each encourages prevention because neither can guarantee being there with the potential victim to perform intervention. It is understood in this society that driver education and responsible driving will help the motorist stay out of trouble. Similarly, crime prevention includes recognition of danger cues, alertness, and responsible behavior. Our society encourages knowledge of first aid so that if there *is* an accident, the first responder can control hemorrhage, stave off shock, and stabilize a fractured leg until the trained, designated professionals get there with their paramedic kits and ambulance to transport the patient to the trauma doc at the hospital. Similarly, our society needs to encourage this same first responder model for private citizen self-defense, and that's what Dave Kenik is talking about. If there *is* a crime of violence, the potential victim needs the wherewithal to stop the deadly danger and stabilize the scene by himself until a separate set of designated, specially-trained and equipped professionals, can get to the scene to do their job.

Dave was an exemplary student at my school, Lethal Force Institute, and it gratifies me to see how much he learned at LFI has been transferred to the pages that follow. Soliciting Ralph Mroz to write the chapter on close combat was typical Kenik smarts and pragmatism. I've known Mroz for many years, starting when he first came to LFI, and Kenik couldn't have picked a better specialist for the topic.

I think Dave Kenik has succeeded admirably in putting together this concise guide for the beginner in the field of armed self-defense. He and I may not agree on every detail, but few experts in any field do. Suffice to say that Dave has packed a lot of good advice in this book, and I think his target audience will find its price to be some of the best money they ever spent.

Currently serving as captain and police prosecutor with a municipal police department in northern New England, Massad Ayoob is the author of what has been called the authoritative text on civilian use of lethal force in self-defense, "In the Gravest Extreme." The winner of the 1998 Outstanding American Handgunner of the Year award, Ayoob is handgun editor of GUNS magazine, law enforcement editor of AMERICAN HANDGUNNER, and associate editor of COMBAT HANDGUNS and GUNS & WEAPONS FOR LAW ENFORCEMENT. He is the director of Lethal Force Institute, PO Box 122, Concord, NH 03302, (800)624-9049, www.ayoob.com.

INTRODUCTION

"I wish I knew what I know now, when I was younger."
Rod Stewart

Carrying a gun takes commitment – a lot of commitment. You need to: learn about firearms, learn to shoot, understand and practice gun safety, learn tactics, comprehend legal issues, practice, clean and store the gun, adjust how you dress and perhaps even change your lifestyle and attitude. Beyond those issues, the study of self-defense also encompasses responsibility, mindset, awareness, control, dominance and discipline. If done right, it's not an avocation to be taken lightly.

The concept of learning about using and carrying guns reminds me of my experience with scuba diving. My first experience was at a resort in Jamaica – one hour lecture, one hour in the pool and the next day I was 60 feet under water. The following year I took a full certification course from a qualified professional instruction facility and quickly learned how dangerous the "resort course" was. Same thing with firearms. The more I learned about firearms, the more I realized how much there is to know and how dangerous it is to not have the knowledge.

The gun is the easy part. It's also the smallest and least significant element of staying safe. Awareness, mindset, and attitude are what will keep you safe. The gun is a tool – just a tool. If trouble finds you, tactics are your most important ally followed by skill with your safety tools. Your true weapon is your mind. A person with a .22 and a plan is far more formidable than a clueless person with a .45.

The best way to win a gunfight is not to be in one. I have trained and carried for over two decades and hope never to put my efforts to the ultimate test. In using lethal force, the worst-case scenario is that you get killed. Best case; you win the gun fight and are embroiled in legal battles – either criminal, to prove you acted in self-defense, and/or civil, where the scumbag's family sues you for violating the criminal's rights by not allowing him to kill you. A defense could easily cost $100,000, even if you were in the right and you win.

Use common sense to avoid locations and situations that increase your risk. Carrying a gun does not eliminate risk. You should not go anywhere or do anything while carrying a gun that you would not do otherwise. It is has been said that people who carry guns are less likely participate in fights. It is not because they have a gun, but because of their awareness that, due to the fact that they have a gun, an altercation could result in a death.

The knowledge, mindset, and tactics needed to win the ultimate fight do not come easy, nor cheap. My road to knowledge was filled with bumps, u-turns, forks and dead ends which I hope to help you circumnavigate.

I wrote this book in the hopes of saving my fellow (and future) shooters from wasting untold dollars and unimaginable time learning what I have learned since I started shooting and carrying guns over two decades ago.

My perspective is not that of a sworn police officer, nor that of a professional firearms instructor. Probably not much different from you, I am just an average citizen on a quest to best protect my family and myself. My experience has shown that often a police officer's or other professional gunslinger's advice does not always translate well to the average shooter. Cops receive department-sponsored training, and don't have to worry about concealed carry issues and the like. Many professional writers and instructors have forgotten what it is like to be a novice, and simply can't relate to our concerns and level of knowledge.

My educational odyssey actually started with a book that I bought while in high school, the venerable "In the Gravest Extreme" by Massad Ayoob. Reading that book whetted my appetite for tactical training and legal knowledge on issues of use of force. The day I finished the book, I decided that, someday, I was going to take a class at Ayoob's Lethal Force Institute in New Hampshire. Although my nearly twenty-year wait was worthwhile, I highly recommend that every gun owner not wait and attend a similar school, as soon as possible, to understand the responsible use of lethal force and the tactics needed to survive a lethal encounter.

Ayoob's eye-opening lessons drew me in further to the quest for additional relevant knowledge. My subsequent studies have taught me more in the last few years that I had learned in twenty. My previous knowledge was mostly gained by reading gun magazines where many of the authors had no idea what they were talking about, and from watching and talking to fellow shooters who probably knew less than I did. I knew that half of the information that I uncovered was useless or wrong, I just didn't always know which half.

Fortunately, I have not been involved in a gunfight and have not been forced to defend my actions in court. My tactical and legal lessons were taken from those that have. This book is a compilation of what I have learned from classes that I attended at some of the leading tactical schools, from conversations with some of the most knowledgeable and respected people in the business, from reading lots of books and articles (by competent authors), and very importantly, from going out to the range, myself, to test tactics and theories.

With this book, I hope to expound the wisdom (the good half) that I have deciphered on the use of guns for self-defense.

David Kenik

One THE MISCONCEPTION OF POLICE PROTECTION

The police have no legal obligation to protect you.

Blunt? Yes, but true. Regardless of the slogan proudly proclaiming "To Protect and Serve", the job of the police is primarily to investigate crimes and attempt to apprehend the perpetrators. 'Protection' of individual citizens is simply not in their job description.

This became abundantly clear to me on a personal level, when my family's safety was imperiled by a death threat from a 'crazy old man'. Late one Friday evening, as the Chairman of a grassroots activist group, I was testifying at the State House on an divisive social issue. Along with myself, several other members of the group were also threatened by the same person. We dutifully reported the threat to the State House Police, but didn't give it much concern, as we figured it was just the ramblings of a feeble old man who had nothing better to do.

Two days later, the office of one of the other threatened parties was burned to the ground. From that point on we took the threat seriously.

When the State House opened on Monday, I went back to the State House Police and notified them of the fire and the possible connection to the person who threatened us. They stated that they had no jurisdiction outside of the State House, and that we needed to report it to the city police. The city police said that they would take a report, but they would not investigate. They suggested that I report it to the police in my town. My local police took a report but also said they couldn't do anything because the person making the threat lived in another town. The perpetrator's home town police said that they wouldn't do anything because the threat happened out of their jurisdiction. This event was the catalyst for change of my wife's opinion on the need to be responsible for one's own safety and the use of guns for personal protection.

On Monday, in addition to visiting the police, I also went to the gun store to purchase a shotgun. Not knowing what, who, or how many I might face, I felt a 12 gauge would be both a better deterrent, and a more efficient home defender than my short-barreled .357 revolver. What do you know… an eight-day waiting period prevented me from protecting my family. Are those who make threats also required to wait eight days in order to carry them out?

Police State
If the job of the police were to protect you as an individual, they would then have to protect all other citizens as well. In that circumstance, everyone would need their own personal police officer following them 24 hours a day. Three-quarters of the populace would be required to be employed as police officers to protect the remaining citizens, each hour of the day and night.

Realistic Expectations
Even if the police did have a duty to protect, could they? Think about the situation you are in right this second. Reading this book at home? At work? On the bus? For the sake of discussion, assume that you just are about to become a victim of a violent crime. Someone just burst in and is about to start shooting. Ask yourself these questions:

- Do I have time to reach the phone and dial 911 before being attacked?

- If I reach the phone, will I have time to tell the police my location (not all 911 systems register the address), and tell the dispatcher of the impending danger before that attacker is upon me?

- If I do reach the police through the 911 system, how long will it take the responding officers to arrive?

- Knowing that it takes less then 2 seconds to draw a gun and fire, will the police be able to arrive and save me before the 2 seconds have elapsed?

I think you get the idea. Even if the job of the police were to include protection, realistic circumstances and logic confirms the proclamation of one of my favorite bumper stickers; "My 1911 is better than your 911".

Government Control
If you believe the gun-grabbing politicians, ordinary citizens do not need to own firearms because the police are charged with the security of the community. With this in mind, they then propagate

ongoing attempts to deprive law-abiding citizens of the ability to protect themselves. Gun control is a nothing short of a power grab to keep politicians and the government in a position to overpower the citizenry. I have always maintained that Tiananmen Square could not happen here because we, as U.S. citizens, are armed.

The government has given itself the power to tax, legislate, and control all aspects of our lives. Driving an automobile is a privilege bestowed upon us by the government. Permits, licenses, zoning boards, and building codes are just a few common examples of a government, by the privileged few, designed to control the masses.

The fundamental legitimate purpose of government is to perform services in mass that are unable to be achieved by individuals. Major road construction is a perfect example of the intended purpose of government. Our government asserts that it needs ever-increasing amounts of our tax money to give food to those too lazy to work, to give health care to those that refuse to buy insurance, and to buy needles for drug addicts. However, they say that they owe no duty to protect honest citizens from crime. Does crime control of the entire country sound like a job for each individual citizen?

The courts, in their infinite wisdom, have consistently ruled that police departments and local governments cannot be held liable for not protecting the citizenry. Get this...they can not even be held accountable if they do not respond to your 911 call for assistance.

The courts believe that allowing citizens to sue the state or local government for performing or failing to perform a given governmental function would lead to limitless numbers of lawsuits. They feel that making the government answerable in court for every decision and action it took would interfere with the operation of government itself. Government employees would start working to avoid lawsuits, rather than serving the public good.[1]

The U.S. Supreme Court, in its landmark decision of *DeShaney v. Winnebago County Department of Social Services*[2] ruled that the Constitution does not require government to protect the citizens from criminal harm. The Court wrote:

> ...*nothing in the language of the Due Process Clause itself requires the State to protect the life, liberty and property of its citizens against invasion by private actors. The Clause is phrased as a limitation on the State's power to act, not as a guarantee of certain*

> *minimal levels of safety and security. It forbids the State*
> *itself to deprive individuals of life, liberty, or property*
> *without "due process of law," but its language cannot*
> *fairly be extended to impose an affirmative obligation on*
> *the State to ensure that those interests do not come to*
> *harm through other means.*[3]

Don't take this chapter as a disparagement of the police or our government. Many, many, honest, hard-working police officers put their lives on the line performing valuable services for our society. By any reasonable standard, the U.S. government is not a tyranny, but it is imperative for each of us to understand the limits of our society and its legal system.

There is no one to protect us. We must take the responsibly for personal safety into our own hands. While politicians attempt to control the masses, ultimately, we must remember that self-defense is not a legal right, it is a human right.

Two THE QUESTION

There is one thing that you have to do before you pick up a gun, and even before you continue reading this book. You have to answer a question.

While it may seem like a simple, short question, in reality it may be one of the most important quandaries that you will ever contemplate.

"Can you take a life?"

More to the point, "If you, or a member of your family, are placed in mortal danger, can you shoot a human being to save them or yourself?"

It is imperative to answer this question **before** you find yourself in that situation. For many, the answer is easily reached. Others will need serious consideration and soul searching before the answer becomes clear. Some will never be able to answer with certainty.

If the answer to 'The Question' is "no", do **not** carry a gun. In this circumstance, chances are that a gun will do you more harm than good. Never carry a gun with the thought that just brandishing it will scare off criminal perpetrators. With your smell of fear emanating, your attacker may very well disarm you in a blink of an eye, and then viciously use your own weapon against you. While displaying a gun or using it as a deterrent (short of shooting) _may_ stop a hostile situation, it will not do so unless the criminal perceives that your gun is backed up with confidence and a willingness and ability to use it. If the brandishing does not stop the attack, you must be prepared to fire the gun.

If your answer to 'The Question' is unclear, do not look for this book or for anyone else to help you resolve the issue. This is a very personal decision that cannot be made under the direction of another. If you are unduly persuaded by an outside influence to carry a gun, you very well may find yourself hesitating at the worst possible moment.

If you have conclusively decided that you can and will use lethal force to protect yourself and your family, you owe it to yourself to get as much training and information as possible. Seek out training on the legal use of force. It is imperative to understand when you can shoot, when you can't, and what level of force response is appropriate for different situations. Unfortunately, this is not a simple task that can be performed once and never repeated. You need to keep these issues and answers constantly in the forefront of your consciousness, so that if you find yourself in the unfortunate position of having to defend yourself, you won't question what you can and cannot do.

Tactical training is a must. Paper punching will make you a better target shooter, but you need to learn and continually practice tactical situations. Use of concealment and cover, verbalization, drawing, engaging multiple targets, moving targets, and moving while shooting are just few skills that are essential to win the fight of your life.

If your answer to 'The Question' is 'yes', read on, learn all you can from as many sources as possible, and practice as often and as effectively as possible.

Three   # RESPONSIBLE USE OF LETHAL FORCE

I am not an attorney and this chapter is not meant as legal advice, merely a discussion of the underlying principles of the legality of self-defense. The principles discussed may or may not apply in every jurisdiction, as every state has their own definition of justifiable self-defense.

*I put this chapter towards the front of this book because of its importance. If is far easier to learn **how** to shoot then it is to learn **when** to shoot. It is in the best interests of the reader to be familiar with and stay abreast of the ever-changing laws of any jurisdiction in which you reside or travel.*

A citizen may use deadly force in self-defense only when they actually and reasonably believe that doing so is necessary to prevent an imminent, unlawful, and otherwise unavoidable threat of death or grave bodily harm to in innocent person.[4]

While that statement may seem innocuous on its surface, burdened with requirements, conditions, exceptions and interpretations, it is far more complex than its simplicity implies.

Each state may apply different definitions and interpretations to the concepts of 'necessary', 'imminent,' and 'unavoidable'. For one example, some states' laws may require you to attempt to escape at all costs before using lethal force, while other states may require a "reasonable" attempt. In some cases state laws go further and do not require retreat in your own home. Complicating matters even more, who knows how a jury would interpret "reasonable" or "unavoidable? Or for that matter, how would a jury interpret "grave bodily harm"? As stated previously, it is vital to understand the legal concepts on the use of lethal force and be aware of laws in your state, and those that you travel in.

Death of a human being at the hands of another, no matter the reason, is homicide. The law, however, distinguishes between levels of homicide:

    Premeditated Murder - defined as coldly planned in advance.

First Degree Murder - has element of malice, act was intentionally evil and/or had criminal intent.

Capital Murder - murder of law enforcement officer or politician during the performance of his duties.

Felony Murder - murder committed during the commission of a felony

Second Degree Murder - denotes that the murder was not planned, but may have happened during the commission of a crime.

Manslaughter - considered not intentional, but an action was with reckless and wanton disregard for human life.

Excusable Homicide - probably should not have killed, but other reasonable people in the same situation may have done the same.

Justifiable Homicide - you were right to kill.

To justify the use of lethal force, your perpetrator **must** have the "ability" to kill or cripple, **and** the "opportunity" to kill or cripple, **and** you must be in immediate or imminent "jeopardy". In other words, lethal force can only be used if there is an immediate and otherwise unavoidable danger of death or grave bodily harm to the innocent.

This is vital. To justify use of lethal force, *all three elements must be present:*

Ability – attacker posses the power to kill or cripple (strength, weapon, etc.)

Opportunity – attacker has the opportunity to kill or cripple (close enough)

Jeopardy – attacker must be in the process of attempting to kill or cripple

You may have a hard time convincing a jury that a feeble person, barely able to walk, brandishing a knife from 15 feet away, possesses the ability to kill or cripple. If someone has the ability, such as possession and the ability to use a knife, and threatens to cut your throat from across the a four lane road, that does **not** constitute the 'opportunity' to kill because of the distance — therefore you are not in 'jeopardy'. The assailant is not within immediate striking distance. Likewise, if that person has a knife, is close to the intended victim, but is not actually in the process of employing the attack, lethal force is **not** justified. To legally use lethal force in defense, your attacker must have the power, **and** the ability, **and** is attempting to kill or cripple.

The law allows private citizens only the use of **equal** force against an attacker — lethal force only against lethal force. That does not mean that you can defend yourself with a firearm only if your opponent has one. A baseball bat used with intent to kill can be just as deadly as a firearm. However, the 'power' and 'ability' to kill or cripple does not only mean possession of an object being used as a weapon, but can also be met in a number of other ways. "Disparity of Force" can be used as an element to justify the use of lethal force if the other elements of 'opportunity' and 'jeopardy' are also present.

Examples of 'Disparity of Force' include:

Force of Numbers – the use of lethal force can be justified if multiple assailants are attacking a single person, or if a large group is attacking a small group.

The "Warren Doctrine" states that *within a gang, any member of the mob shares the responsibility for causing reasonable fear. After all but one of the gang are disabled, the last standing is no longer part of a gang[5].*

This means that lethal force is justified against any member of a gang that has ability, opportunity, and presents jeopardy. The last remaining person can no longer be thought of as part of a gang, but needs to be considered based on his own actions.

Able-bodied Against the Disabled – An element of disparity of force includes the attack of a frail person by a healthy person.

Male vs. Female – A man attacking a woman is generally considered to be a disparity of force due to typically overpowering strength.

Size/Weight and **Size/Strength** – A person of greater size and/or strength presents disparity of force.

Attacker of Known Fighting Skill – Disparity of force may be found to exist if it is known to the victim that the attacker has knowledge of specialized fighting skills such as martial arts, boxing, military training in hand-to-hand combat, etc. This assumes that the victim does not have equivalent fighting skills and that the victim is aware of the attacker's knowledge at the time of the altercation. Learning of the attackers fighting skill *after* the altercation is not sufficient to support 'disparity of force' since the victim did not have the knowledge of the attacker's skill at the time. However, if the aggressor's actions demonstrates fighting knowledge, such as taking the posture or stance of someone trained in martial arts, it is possible to argue that a reasonable and prudent person would conclude that the aggressor was trained in fighting skills.

Even if your perpetrator(s) does not have a formal weapon, you can use lethal force if one of the above 'disparity of force' elements exists along with 'opportunity' and 'jeopardy'.

In most jurisdictions, to be justified in using force for the purposes of self-defense, the victim must be *innocent* of provoking the actions that started the altercation. The law does not allow the instigator to claim self-defense in an altercation he started. An example would be if a criminal attacks an innocent victim, and the victim draws a weapon for defense. The criminal can not then claim self-defense in using force against the true victim.

To justify the use of lethal force you **need** more than 'mere suspicion,' you **need** 'articulate suspicion'. You need to be able to articulate a specific threat with certainly. "I thought..." will get you an introduction to Bubba, your cell mate and new best friend. It is essential to be able to state the exact danger that you were in and why you felt you were in that danger. Example: "The attacker showed a behavior consisting of (fill in the crime) that indicated the intention to kill me or inflict grave bodily harm upon me."

To be justified, the use of lethal force also needs to be 'necessary', and 'reasonable'. If the danger is not imminent, lethal force is not justified. (jeopardy). If the knife-wielding maniac is across the street, lethal force is not justified (opportunity). Lethal force used against a seven year old with a baseball bat may not be considered justified (ability). In layman's terms, it boils down to: was the use of lethal force necessary to avoid grave bodily harm or death, or was a reasonable alternative action available?

If you win the gunfight, but lose in court, you go to jail — this can happen even if the use of lethal force was justified. If you are involved in an assault, even as a victim who fights back, expect to be arrested, charged, and later sued. In order to prevail in court, you must understand that your guilt or innocence does **not** matter. The only thing that matters is the jury's *perception* of your guilt or innocence.

When it comes to the legal battle, what your perception of the danger was, the timeline of the struggle at which you began to protect yourself, how you handled yourself during the assault, how you defended yourself, what you said to the police when they arrived, and what you say and how you speak in court are probably as important, if not more important, than the act of violence perpetrated against you by the attacker. If you think defending yourself against an act of violence can't land you in jail, just ask the many people who, while protecting themselves, were perceived as having overstepped the boundaries and are now serving hard time.

Perception *is* reality.

Even if you do everything right, the jury needs to *believe* that you did. You need to be able to articulate the reasons that you felt that you were in danger.

In court, expect your statements to be twisted, the truth to be distorted, the jury to be misinformed and even lied to — and that's just from the prosecutor. Expect even more despicable actions if you face the perpetrator's attorney in a civil case.

If your acts were that of self-defense, your only responsible position in court is that of an **affirmative defense**. Admit your action, with reasonable and justifiable reasons. — "Yes, I shot him because he was about to (fill in violent act) and I concluded that he meant to kill me. I did what was necessary to stop him." If your testimony is something like you were startled, which then caused you to unintentionally fire your gun, say hello to cell mate Bubba.

It is vital to understand your rights and what constitutes justification, because courts do not allow an excuse for an act if it can be shown that you were not aware of the justifying reason at the time. Example: in order to use the Tueller Drill that demonstrates that "a person can transverse a distance of 21 feet in an average of 1.5 seconds" as part of your defense, you must be able to show that you knew that fact before you were attacked. (Refer to the chapter: "Action beats Reaction" for more information on the Tueller Drill.)

Retreat

One scale to measure justification of lethal force is to consider if the action was necessary and unavoidable. Was the victim *able* to escape? Did the victim choose to fight *rather than* escape?

Retreat from a fight, if it is possible to be done safety, is **always** preferable to engaging in lethal force. The object of a gunfight is to go home — even if that means apologizing when you were not wrong, admitting to your attacker that you are afraid to fight, or by running away. A fight never fought, is a fight won. The absolute last thing you want to do is engage is a firefight. Just because you draw a gun, does not mean you are going to win without paying a penalty — you may still get injured, go to jail, and/or get sued. If you loose, you may get killed, or injured or end up in jail.

Many states have adopted the 'Castle Doctrine', which states that a defender need not retreat if attacked in his dwelling (castle), even if he could do so in complete safety. Some court decisions even afford the Castle Doctrine to places of business. Legal requirements vary wildly from state to state, so it is imperative to know what your rights and responsibilities are.

Escalation

As previously stated, citizens are legally allowed to protect themselves with force **equal** to that of their aggressor. Lethal force may be used only against lethal force. If you are the party who escalates the force level, you will be considered the aggressor. An example would be a verbal argument. The person who first uses physical force would be considered the aggressor, and the person who is physically assaulted is considered the victim. If you get mad and punch the person you are arguing with, you become the bad guy, even if he started the verbal altercation.

If the person you are fighting with then engages you with a weapon, and it was judged that his action was not a reasonable response, he is the one responsible for the escalation and now becomes the aggressor. Your actions determine if the jury sees you as the innocent victim or the assailant.

Re-engagements

Similar to escalation issues, re-engagement after an altercation has ended can change your role as a victim to that of an aggressor. If the aggressor retreats, the fight is over. If you then attack the aggressor, you have started a second, separate fight and now you are the assailant. It does not matter what preceded the fight, it only matters who started the altercation and who escalated it.

Right of Pursuit

Unlike a police officer, an ordinary citizen does not have the right to pursue a criminal. Pursuit, by definition, means that the criminal has ceased his criminal behavior and has fled. Going after a fleeing criminal after the crime has concluded is considered re-engagement.

Defense of Others

Most states allow the use of lethal force in the defense of another so long as the use of force reasonably appears to be justified. Again, the laws of every state vary. A good rule of thumb is to put yourself in the 'victim's' place and use only equal force. Use lethal force only if all elements of ability, opportunity, and jeopardy are present.

In the case of defending a third party, you must be extremely cognizant of the fact that you may not know all of the details of the altercation. The person you are about to 'save' may actually be the assailant. You would have no way of knowing this unless you were witness to the onset of the proceeding altercation. If you come across a victim being mugged by two men, it could, in fact, be two undercover police officers affecting a legal arrest. If you observe a man with a gun running out of a convenience store, and someone follows yelling "Stop him, he just shot someone," the running man with the gun may very well be the victim of a robbery seeking help, and the person who yelled to have him stopped may be the criminal seeking to create a diversion for extra escape time. Be sure you know **all** of the facts before using force.

Defense of Property

Many concealed carry licenses/permits state right on the document that the purpose of issue is for "protection of life and property." This can be grossly misleading, as almost all states prohibit the use of lethal force for defense of property. Once again, lethal force can be used only when facing an imminent threat of death or grave bodily harm.

TIP: If you are in the unfortunate position of having to defend your actions in court, it will probably be necessary to demonstrate what specialized knowledge you have and when you gained that knowledge since knowledge acquired after the fact can not be used as part of your defense. For instance, to use the fact that the

Tueller Drill demonstrated that an attacker can transverse 21 feet in an average of 1.5 seconds, (see chapter 7 for more information) you need to be able to prove that you knew about the Tueller Drill *before* the attack against you. To prove what specific knowledge you learned and when you gained that knowledge, make detailed notes of all relevant class lectures, videos, books and magazine articles and mail a copy of them to yourself in a certified letter. Leave the notes sealed in the envelope with the dated postmark of the U.S. Postal Service. If needed, the envelope can be opened in court to prove what knowledge you possessed at a given date.

*I cannot stress enough that the use of lethal force is an area of concern that **every** gun owner should be **thoroughly** knowledgeable in. For more information, I suggest the following books:*

"In the Gravest Extreme" by Massad Ayoob, published by Police Bookshelf.

"The Law of Self-Defense: A Guide for the Armed Citizen" by Andrew F. Branca, published by Operon Security, Ltd.

Four   # PROPERTIES OF
                          # SURIVAL

In order to survive a threat, three primary elements need to work together. First and foremost, you need to become aware of the threat. The threat then needs to be assessed and finally, you must decide upon and carry out the appropriate response.

AWARENESS

To be able to identify a threat, you must maintain a constant vigilance of mental awareness. Without awareness, the best gun, the most powerful ammunition, and the all of the tactical training in the world will be useless. If unaware of your surroundings, you

Stay cognizant of where a criminal can enter and what your egress options are.

are unprepared to react — a recipe for the perpetrator to prevail. A 'surprise attack' may not be a surprise if you are aware of your surroundings.

While walking from the store to your car, are you oblivious to your surroundings, or are you alert to other pedestrians and cars? Did you see the person lurking behind the tree? Did you check your back seat before entering your car? Do you look at the interior mirrors before entering an elevator?

As with many other things, there are various levels of awareness — from complete lack of awareness of your surroundings and situation, to being under direct attack. The U.S. military color codes are used to categorize and describe levels of awareness. It is useful to understand the levels, not only as a definition, but also as a guide to what levels of awareness are appropriate for different situations.

The awareness color codes are:

> **White** – unprepared for violence, not alert to symptoms or signs of violence. Going about your own business in an ignorant daze. Many car accidents happen because drivers are in condition white.

Yellow – relaxed alertness. Not tense or nervous, but maintaining mental awareness of surroundings and possible intent of others. Alertness of surroundings would include such things as looking at your surroundings and noticing who is present as you walk down the street and knowing lanes of egress in every situation you find yourself in.

Orange – perception of an unspecified threat, but of unknown nature. An example would be the sound of glass breaking, which could indicate a burglar or just a cat knocking something over. This heightened state of alert causes 'Body Alarm Reaction' which increases pulse rate, blood pressure, and breathing. Ready your weapons and take immediate note of concealment, cover, and lanes of egress,

Red – this threat level means that there is a perceived and deliberate danger to you. With a direct threat, immediately take cover, draw weapon, control egress, and use verbalization to engage and challenge the threat.

Black – This level corresponds to a direct lethal assault in progress, a non-negotiable situation. This action causes the need to neutralize the situation by shooting to stop the attacker.

Benefits of Awareness

Situational awareness encompasses several main elements: looking for potential attackers, knowing the locations of cover and concealment, finding exits and seeking lanes of egress.

Being aware of your situation and surroundings can benefit you threefold. 1) You can escape trouble by simply avoiding it. If you are watching your surroundings and you see

Being aware means looking for cover and concealment options wherever you are. Here, telephone poles, trees, cars, houses, and masonry walls offer lots of options.

what looks like trouble ahead, stay clear. 2) Knowing about trouble ahead of time can give you time to prepare a plan, seek out cover and concealment, and ready your weapons (retrieve pepper spray, open your knife, place hand on gun, etc.) 3) If the assailant knows that you are aware of his presence and possibly prepared for an encounter, he may simply decide to find an easier victim.

Criminals most often don't select a victim at random. They seek an opponent they can beat readily. They would rather take $10 from an easy victim then fight with a victim over $50. In the 1960s, street thugs would often seek out hippies to victimize, since they would surrender their valuables without a struggle, and would not report the crime to police. Today, nothing has changed — criminals seek victims who are unaware and unprepared. They seek those living in condition 'white'. Natives of New York City call people who look up at the skyscrapers, 'tourists' — criminals call them victims.

All too many people exist in a state of "white". I also refer to this as 'ignorant bliss'. It is best to be aware of your surroundings at all times — remain vigilant and alert. You can live your entire life in 'yellow' without any psychological harm whatsoever. Condition 'yellow' tells the stalking criminal who is watching you that you are aware of your surroundings and you are probably aware of his presence. The assailant will get a sense that you are not the easy victim he seeks.

Being alert does not mean that you are paranoid. Wherever you are, be aware of others. Look for indications of their intentions. Are they simply walking to their car, or are they looking inside every car they pass? Widen your vision. Don't concentrate on just what is in front of you, but also what surrounds you. Note possible concealment and cover. If someone were to burst out shooting right this instant, what would you do? Where would you hide? How would you escape? What would you do to stop the attack?

THREAT ASSESSMENT

Before you can determine your response to a perceived threat, you must understand the level of jeopardy facing you. Threat assessment can be the most difficult survival element, both because the attacker may mask his true intentions and the severity of the potential harm may not yet be evident.

An assailant might threaten you with grave bodily harm but point a water pistol. A mugger may say that you will not be hurt if you hand over your wallet, but then stab you as you reach to give it to him.

As difficult as it may be to determine, your response needs to be appropriate to the perceived threat level. If you overreact, you could land in jail. If you don't react or under-react you could land six feet under. Start your assessment by determining if the danger is a direct threat to you. Your response will differ

Will he shoot or let you go?

significantly depending on the circumstances. If threatened directly with gunfire, take cover, draw your weapon and return fire if appropriate. If you hear a random gunshot and are not in direct danger, take cover, then get out of the area as soon as it is feasible and as fast as possible. Keep in mind that to draw a weapon in this situation may put you in mortal danger.

A police officer or concerned citizen (like you!) may see you with a drawn gun and assume that *you* are the criminal. Remember — the purpose of the firearm is to get you *out* of trouble, not into it.

Presuming that you are faced with a direct threat, is it a lethal threat? Does the perpetrator want to simply punch you, or beat you with a baseball bat? In order to respond with lethal force, you must be facing an imminent threat of death or grave bodily harm. You generally cannot use more force than you are threatened with. (See previous chapter on 'Responsible Use of Lethal Force')

Does the perpetrator have the ability to carry out the threat and is the threat imminent? Are you being threatened with a knife from across a wide street, or is the attacker just 20 feet away and closing? A knife threat from 50 feet is not a lethal threat, while the same threat with a gun could be considered lethal. If you are being threatened with a gun, is the gun being drawn, or is the threat not viable because the perpetrator does not have the gun in his hand?

Are you just being verbally threatened, or is the attack in progress? If you are threatened as intimidation, you **do not** have the right to use lethal force because you are not in immediate jeopardy of loosing your life or suffer grave bodily harm.

ELEMENTS OF RESPONSE

Most shooters that I have come in contact with are far more concerned about the choice of gun, caliber, and cartridge than they are with tactics. In reality, the type of gun and ammunition are almost unimportant. How you use what you have is far more important.

The elements of response in order of importance are:
- proper tactics
- skill with defensive weapon
- the proper choice of weapon

The order of importance is very telling. Tactics (what you do) are more important than how you do it and what you do it with. Tactics means being aware of your situation and surroundings, knowing what skills to apply and how to apply them. Tactics means understanding such things as knowing where you are in relation to cover and how to get to the closest door. It means understanding how to transverse a doorway and how to flank your opponent. The ability to hit the 10 ring of a paper target is not important if you are dead before you pull your gun out.

Tactics also includes avoiding a situation when you perceive a threat. If you see a threat on the sidewalk ahead of you, why not just cross the road and place yourself out of the person's reach? It is far better to avoid trouble than dealing with it after it starts.

Once you have applied the proper tactics, skill in the use of your chosen weapon, (shooting, in the case of a firearm), is the next most important element. While I dislike repeating clichés, these are appropriate:

"A hit with a 9mm is better than a miss with a .45."

"A slow hit is better than a fast miss."

Simply stated, shot placement is far more important than what bullet you are shooting or what gun you are shooting.

What is lost on many people is that the choice of gun and ammunition is actually the least important element of survival. The smallest gun in the hands of an aware, prepared, and skilled person is much more effective than the largest gun in the hands of a person who is unprepared to present a proper defense. The number one element of survival is awareness. Once an attack has commenced, proper use of tactics will give you an opportunity to survive. A series of well-placed rounds should stop the attack.

Five # BODY ALARM
REACTION

If you are ever in the unfortunate situation of being in a lethal force encounter, your body will be in a heightened state of alarm and will react with chemical and physiological changes.

When sensing danger, Body Alarm Reaction (BAR) subconsciously takes over. Under perceived threat, the body, using its natural instinct to survive, produces an adrenal dump that causes increases in pulse rate, blood pressure, and breathing. It also amplifies strength and situational concentration. While those reactions are good for the physical body, they create various physical consequences which can be distracting and harmful if you don't know that they are imminent. The good news is that by understanding them, you can counteract them and fight through them.

Physical BAR responses can include tunnel vision, auditory exclusion, decreased dexterity in extremities (especially fingers), impaired thinking, and a distorted sense of time and distance.

Everyone has already experienced BAR in some form or another. That sick feeling in your stomach and chest that instantly occurs when you are involved in a near miss automobile accident is BAR. Not everyone will experience all BAR reactions and the intensity will vary for each individual. While these responses sound debilitating, as I said, understanding them will lessen their effects and will enable you to fight through them.

Tunnel vision will restrict your vision to the threat at hand and

 auditory exclusion will reduce your hearing. You may hear nothing, or you might hear your adversary and nothing else. Many people report not even hearing the sound of their own gun. The danger in this is obvious. Being oblivious to your surroundings may allow a second criminal to flank you, or you may not hear the commands of a police officer attempting to intervene. To mitigate

these responses after you are involved in a shooting, and the bad guy is neutralized, keep your gun on the threat and do a visual scan. If you have a safety or a decocker, engage it. Lower your gun slightly so you can see over it. Look to the right, then back to the threat. Look to the left, then back to the threat. Once the initial scan is done, do it again, looking farther around and further away. Make threat-scanning part of your practice routine. Every

Lower the gun just enough to see over it and threat scan in both directions.

time you finish shooting a string in practice, threat scan before holstering in order to make it second nature.

Decreased dexterity in your extremities will reduce your ability to perform fine motor skills. That means that you probably won't even be able to feel that your finger is on the trigger, and manipulating a small mechanism such as a slide stop may be impossible. While we can't change those effects, training can help overcome them. Train with gross movements: instead of using that tiny slide stop, use a gross movement to grip the slide from the rear to rack it for loading. It may take two hands to manipulate devices such as safeties and magazine

Actuating the slide stop is a fine motor skill that will be diminished with the effects of BAR.

The gross movement of racking the slide will be easier to perform under the influence of BAR.

catch releases. Highly honed motor skills and high competence through training will enable you to overcome the effect of reduced dexterity.

Increased pulse rate, blood pressure, and breathing will most likely make your body shake. The good news is that at combat distances, the shaking will not affect your ability to hit the target. I did not believe it myself until I tried it. Stand 10 feet or so from a target and shake your hands while shooting to simulate your body's reaction. While the group size certainly opens up, even with shaking, accuracy at combat distances is good enough. It is a good idea to regularly practice this to create confidence for when it happens for real.

Distorted sense of time and distance will do crazy things to your recollection of events. Time may seem to slow down dramatically or speed up excessively. You may think you are 30 feet apart, when in reality you may only be standing 8 feet away. While these effects cannot be mitigated, it is imperative to understand them when making statements to the responding police. As I discuss in the "Consequences of a Shooting" chapter, it is imperative not to give the police any statements at the time of the shooting for this exact reason. You don't want to tell them that you heard one gunshot when five were fired, and you don't want to tell them you were 30 feet away from your adversary when in really you were much closer. Your distorted memory can get you in trouble. That's why it is imperative to inform the responding officers **only** that the perpetrator attacked you and tried to kill you and you had to defend yourself. Advise them that you wish to seek counsel with an attorney before making a statement.

A Providence Rhode Island tragedy was possibly the result of the effects of Body Alarm Reaction. Officer Cornel Young, an off-duty, rookie police officer, intervened in an altercation involving firearms outside of a restaurant that he was in at about 2 am. Responding officers found a man with his gun aimed at two people involved in a fight, and did not recognize him as it was dark and Officer Young was dressed in a hooded sweatshirt, backlit by a streetlight. Not recognizing that Young was a fellow police officer, the two responding officers ordered Young three times to drop his weapon. Young then turned towards the officers, pointing his gun at them, and was fatally shot by the police. The shooting was ruled as justified because the victim did not identify himself as a police officer, refused three orders to drop his gun, and then pointed the gun at the officers when turning towards them.

While we will never know, I believe that the effects of Body Alarm Reaction caused this terrible chain of events. It is my theory that tunnel vision kept Officer Young from knowing that police officers had arrived on the scene, and that auditory exclusion kept him from hearing the police officers' orders to drop his gun. When Young turned his head towards to the police officers to see what was happening, his body naturally turned with him, aiming his gun towards the police and triggering his fatal shooting. If Officer Young had realized that he may not be seeing and hearing everything, and had he threat scanned with his gun pointing towards the real threat instead of letting it follow his head movements towards the police, events may have had a very different ending.

It is important to realize the effects that Body Alarm Reaction will produce. The way to overcome BAR is through understanding and training. Develop confidence and competence through training, practice visualization of what to do in a lethal situation and trust your trained instincts.

Six HYPE AND HYPERBOLE

As I stated in my introduction, I think that half of what I read or hear is not correct, but I am not always sure *which* half. That goes for guns, cars, news, and just about anything else you can think of. Other than in the handful of "true" consumer review magazines, when did you read an article about how bad a particular new car was? Have you ever seen a stereo magazine report that a new CD player was not worth buying? Did any of the computer magazines advise you to stay away from a particular model?

I suspect that your answer to these questions is "no". The reason that we so rarely see a critical review is that the media industry is built on hype. The foundation and structure is run on profits generated by advertising paid for by the very companies whose products are being reviewed, and they will not tolerate bad press. The meaning to you and I is that most of what we read is highly biased and suspect.

Unfortunately, much of what we read about firearms follows the same track. What we read in non-product related articles, such as on tactics and training, may not be as feasible in the real world as indicated in the articles and videos. I can think of a few reasons for this: the author honestly believes the technique or suggestion is viable; the author never put the technique to test in a realistic scenario; or the author likes to see his name in print. Unfortunately, more than few of the 'top' writers in the industry are more concerned about the paycheck from each article than the factual and practical basis that their information should be founded on. On the other hand, some extremely competent trainers only rarely get their work in print, mostly because they insist on "telling it like it is," which is not always what advertisers want.

It is up to you to verify the conclusions of any article or training concept. While it may be expensive and time consuming to do so, the alternative may be far more costly.

For the selection of firearms, most articles will do a good job covering features, but you should use them only as a starting point. Rarely do they discuss manufacturing quality, or the fact that the fit and feel will be different for every user. Try to borrow a gun before buying. Seek out friends that may have the model you are interested in. Ask people at the range. Most people are more than willing to share their experiences with their guns and even let you shoot them. Gun owners are a friendly bunch, and I have never been turned down when I asked to try someone's gun. It is polite to use your own ammunition or offer to pay for theirs. I have even gone so far to announce at a gun club meeting that I was looking for someone who had a particular gun. If you can't find one to borrow, many ranges offer a rental service. If you can't borrow or rent, you will be forced to buy. While there are many things that I will not buy used, I will happily buy used firearms, since not much can go wrong with a lightly used firearm. If it is in need of repair or adjustment, a trip to a gunsmith can take care of the issues. This is not to say that all used

Find a gun store with a wide variety of guns to see which model and size fits you best.

firearms are in perfect shape, but chances are that if it looks like it has been rarely used, it probably has been. I have seen many used guns that look like new, but that are priced significantly lower than new. All other things being equal, I would prefer to buy used and spend the savings on ammunition. Unfortunately, I have purchased firearms then decided to sell them because it turned out that they did not fit my needs. Buying a less-expensive used gun in the first place certainly takes much of the sting out of selling it later if you decide to.

While the workings of a gun are rather cut and dry, tactics and training methods are not. Don't believe anything that you read or see unless you try it yourself. Many techniques and products don't work as advertised, many look good in articles or videos but don't work at realistic speeds, some are just plain bad advice, and even worse, some are almost willfully wrong.

One article I recently read extolled the virtues of a new belt design with an integrated holster that was intended for carry purposes. The belt was manufactured from two bands of leather sewn together, leaving about a 5-inch opening between the leather bands on each side so a that a gun can be slipped it. The supposed advantage was that when you take the gun out, it looked like an ordinary belt. There are three well-known flaws in that design concept;

1. Not being molded nor fit to the gun, there was nothing to prevent the gun from slipping out.

2. The barrel of the gun was exposed beneath the belt, which allows the possibility of the front sight getting stuck as a draw is attempted.

3. Since the belt collapsed by design, the shooter would be unable to safely and easily reholster, possibly creating a danger in a tactical situation.

This example of irresponsible journalism disturbs me greatly because the problems with the design are not based on one person's opinion, but on well-accepted issues. The writer either chose to ignore the issues or was ignorant of them. In either case, it calls into question the experience, knowledge, and integrity of both the author, and the publication that printed the article.

Defense against a knife attack is just one of the skills that is much more difficult to do in real life than is typically presented.

Some techniques look good in an article but bear little resemblance to reality. In particular, discussions on hands-on techniques, such as defending against a knife, disarming, and close-quarters shooting, are often not as effective in real time as they are portrayed in publications. Demonstrations look great when they are done in slow motion, but the dynamics in a real fight don't work the same.

Ralph Mroz, martial artist, gun writer, knife writer, police officer, and author of the "Empty Hands Self-Defense" chapter of this book, has studied hands-on techniques in a variety of disciplines. His overall conclusion is that many techniques are all but impossible to perform on anyone who isn't cooperating. He goes further by postulating "Mroz's Law," which states "Anything will work at half speed and half force. Most things will work at three-quarters speed and three-quarters force, a surprising number of things will work at seven-eighths speed and seven-eighths force, but almost nothing will work at full speed and full force".[6] This leads us back again to the fact that we need to test every conclusion ourselves.

When testing a gun, don't just target shoot at a bullseye target, test as you would carry, and how you might shoot in a real life situation. Guns feel different in the store compared to riding in your holster in a tactical situation. When I first picked up Para Ordinance's LDA at the gun store, it felt great. Getting it out on the range and drawing from a holster at full speed proved that the trigger reach was too long for my relatively short fingers. The moral is 'test as you would shoot.' Use full speed draws from your carry holster (only after practicing and training yourself on the new gun in slow motion), use carry ammunition not lightweight practice reloads, engage multiple targets with multiple shots, move and use cover. The only way to get the true feeling of a gun is to use all of the practice techniques you can think of, in as much of a realistic situation as possible.

For holsters, test them with the gun you will be using, and the concealment garments that you will wear. I have heard wonderful things about ankle holsters, mostly by the manufacturers of ankle holsters themselves. To prove or disprove their claims, I needed to test them myself. I tested the concealability of ankle holsters simply by looking at my leg. For two days, every time that I stood up, sat down, got in my car, or did similar movements, I looked at my ankle to see the position of my pants. On more than just a few occasions, my pant leg was raised high enough to expose a holster if I had one on. Concealability in real life was not what it was cracked up to be. Testing the draw of an ankle holster in the car saw revealed similar conclusions.

For deep concealment holsters, wear them with normal clothes and day-to-day situations, and test your ability and the time it takes to draw an unloaded gun from them. (As always, test with unloaded guns, double-checking to be sure). Can you draw while running? How fast can you really draw while sitting, and how does it compare to the speed of a realistic attack?

Some techniques require fine movements, but under attack fine motor control and feeling in your extremities will disappear. Will the technique work when your heart is beating two times normal, hands are shaking, and your mind is working in slow motion? The only way to know is to duplicate the situation as closely as possible. While you can't create the Body Alarm Reaction of a lethal threat, simulate an attack as close as possible in real time to test the technique. For years, I used the thumb of my non-dominant hand to release the slide lock of my pistol during a reload. That was until I missed it twice during a stressful reload in an IPSC match, due to loss of fine motor control and feelings in my fingers. I have since changed techniques and now grab the rear of the slide with my support hand, a technique that uses gross movements rather than fine. You won't know until you test. (See Chapter 5 on Body Alarm Reaction for more information)

My last example is from a class that I took on knife defense. We were taught to block the incoming knife by deflecting the arm. Like Mroz's Law said, it worked great in slow motion, but when it was done at full speed the fake knife hit me almost before I could see it coming.

Believe nothing you see or read, including what you read here, until you have tested it for yourself. To separate fact from fiction, think about every technique in detail, figure out its strengths and weaknesses and test it in real time, with full power. You will be astonished how many products and techniques don't work when put to the test. So much so, I just had to write a book!

Seven ACTION BEATS REACTION

The laws of physics state that "for every action, there is an equal but opposite reaction." In the world of self-defense the rule is "Action beats reaction", and there is nothing equal about them.

The time it takes to realize that an aggressor's body is in motion, assess its threat factor, determine a response, and actually have your body respond is astoundingly long. Every time I see myself perform with a delayed reaction, I am further amazed and dismayed as to the time it took to react. Recently, I watched my son fall a short distance off the back of a toy car. It took almost until he hit the floor for my body to start to move towards him, even though I clearly saw him lose his grip and start to lean backwards.

One of the first to realize how this relates to self-defense, test reaction time, and relate it to firearms for self-defense was Dennis Tueller with the Detective Division of the Salt Lake City Police Department (ret.). The lesson of his "Tueller Drill" has become standard fare for tactical schools and there is much legal precedent for its use as a defense in court.[7] First published in 1983, the Tueller drill assesses the lethal threat posed by a contact-type weapon (knife, club, etc.) utilized at distance. It answers the question as to whether or not a pocket knife or other impact weapon in the hands of an assailant can be considered a lethal weapon if the perpetrator is further away than contact distance.

In short, the drill puts an assailant 21 feet from the intended victim. On signal, the assailant's run to the victim is timed, as is the victim's draw. Through the use of this drill by a wide variety of ages, weights, physical abilities, and sizes of people, it was determined that the average time that it takes to transverse 21 feet is 1.5 seconds. The average time that it takes to recognize the threat, draw, and fire is closer to 2 seconds for average shooters. The significance of this conclusion is that a pocketknife or other impact weapon may be legally considered a lethal weapon when the perpetrator is 21 feet away and the victim's gun is in its holster.

The Tueller Drill also goes far in its efforts to shed light on physical reaction time. Not many of my friends or associates, even the ones who carry, believe that someone with an impact weapon 21 feet away is a threat at all, never mind that they can pose a truly lethal threat. They are in for a rude awakening if they ever find themselves in that unfortunate situation. I mention this as an impetus for you to set up the drill and try it yourself.

In a recent instructor certification course, we ran the drill with live fire. To stay safe, the assailant ran in the opposite direction of the gunfire. When the victim felt the assailant's hand leave his shoulder, he raised the gun from a low ready position and fired two shots. Results showed that the assailant was able to travel about 17 feet before the first shot was fired and was beyond 21 feet when the second shot was fired — and this was with very experienced shooters from a low ready position, not even from a holster! This shows that even with the gun in hand, you may very well get stabbed by an assailant who is 17 feet away when he starts his attack. What is even scarier, is that with forward momentum, even a few good shots may not stop the attack. It is well established that even after a fatal wound to the attacker, his body can retain enough oxygenated blood to allow up to 14 seconds of continued movement. In the case of an attacker running towards you, step sideways out of the line of movement or backwards to create distance while firing.

Don't try just the Tueller Drill, try other realistic scenarios and test your reaction time. Use this information to devise training scenarios and develop mental awareness of what the reality of a lethal situation is.

Here are a few suggested scenarios to mock-up and test:

In a convenience store, you walk up to the counter from the back of the store to find a clerk held at gunpoint. Fearing he will kill the clerk, you draw your weapon and order the criminal to put down his gun. Can you shoot him before he turns 90 degrees towards you and fires?

You are driving in your car and accidentally hit the car in front of you. In a violent rage the driver of the car you just hit bursts from his car and runs to you with a hammer in hand. Can you draw before he gets close enough to smash your window

Test how long it takes to get to your gun in this type of situation.

and attack you?

You are awakened in the middle of the night to the noise of someone breaking in your front door. Can you get your family to a defendable location and retrieve your firearm from your quick-action safe before the assailant reaches you or your family? What if you are watching TV in the living room during a home invasion?

You are walking through a parking lot to your car and are approached by two thugs brandishing knives and threatening you. Can you draw before they stab you?

You are in the middle of a fistfight, started by your adversary, and it turns lethal. Your opponent yells that he is going to kill you, picks up a chair and heads towards you. Can you draw before getting hit with the chair?

Use these and other mock scenarios to see what your options really are. Use the results to adjust your plan. If you can't get your family together and reach your firearm before someone can get to you, figure out what you can

There may be no time to get to your gun in a direct attack.

change to give yourself a better chance. Perhaps a different meeting place for the family? Perhaps a different location for the gun?

When your tests demonstrate that you will not be able to shoot the assailant before he shoots you, change your tactical thought process and don't put yourself in that position. Use the lessons learned to change your behavior — both everyday behavior and your tactical techniques. I started carrying at home when I realized that someone could break into any door in my single level home and get to me or my family well before I could reach my quick-action gun safe. While some may think carrying at home is paranoid, how else could a home invasion be stopped?

No one would suspect that your hand is on a pistol, ready for action.

In areas with other people, especially locations like parking lots, I walk with my hand in my pocket, on the grip of my pocket gun. Not only does this offer a far faster draw, it offers me the element of surprise, since no one would expect me to pull out a gun.

I can't express enough how important it is to understand the slowness of reaction time and how it affects survivability. Testing and experimentation will enable you to dramatically alter your perception of what you can and cannot accomplish, and will offer insights on how you need to change your thought process and techniques to increase your chances of survival.

Lastly, one of conclusions implied by the results of the Tueller drill is that empty hands defense skills are vital, as you may well need to fend off the attack with your bare hands before you can engage with a firearm. The next chapter, by Ralph Mroz, further emphasizes this need.

Eight # THE NEED FOR EMPTY HAND SKILLS

by Ralph Mroz

1. The foundation of **all** self-defense skills is empty hands skills.

2. No matter what weapons(s) you carry and are trained with, you are still most likely going to have to depend on empty hands skills at some level for **any** type of attack.

The first statement comes as a shock to many people who feel that if they carry a gun or pepper spray, then they are adequately prepared to defend themselves in a threatening encounter. The second statement may seem counter-intuitive, in that we are saying that even lethal force attacks are likely to have to be met with your bare hands.

Neither statement is comfortable. Both are true.

Statement one is true in that all weapons skills are physical in their nature. They all depend on your ability to move surely, and with balance and coordination, and even possibly with power. These attributes come from developing empty hand skills, martial arts or defensive tactics, call them what you will, like no other method can. Further, no matter what the weapon you are attempting to access in response to a threat, you will probably be starting from behind the power curve — that is, your attacker has probably surprised you and you are reacting to his movements. Therefore, you will probably need to

If attacked at close range, you will be behind the power curve and won't have time to reach for a weapon.

ward off the attack with your empty hands, before, or at best at the same time that you are accessing your weapon.

The second statement is true in that you are reacting to your attacker's initiation of the assault. Your weapon cannot be brought to bear until you have crossed the time frames of your reaction time and your weapon presentation time. Reaction times vary from 0.25 seconds for a highly trained athlete **who is alert** to an imminent cue, to more than a second for less trained people in other states of awareness. You have to then add your draw and presentation time to that if you are accessing a handgun. The time frames we are talking about here total about one to two seconds, for a person who is expecting an assault cue. The way this is measured is in one of the classic training exercises for handguns: the shooter stands facing an 8-inch steel plate (about the size of the area you need to hit on an attacker to have a good chance of stopping him), waiting for a buzzer to sound. At the buzzer, the shooter draws and fires on the plate. Extremely good times (from a speed holster, and not drawing from concealment) are in the sub-second range. Typical times for **good** shooters are in the 1 to 1.7 seconds range. If you are not practiced in this exercise, if you are drawing from concealment, or you are drawing from anything but an open-top holster (a so-called "speed scabbard"), then add additional time. If you are surprised by the attack, or you are trying to perform another action in addition to the draw (like getting the heck out of there or warding off the attack), then add even more time.

Now consider how much time it takes for the assailant to strike you, knife you, or shoot you. As we saw from the Tueller Drill in the previous chapter, it is only a fraction of a second.

The bottom line is that in a typical attack you simply don't have time to access your handgun before you are injured. Your only hope is to first deal with the attack, whatever its nature, with your empty hands. It's simply a matter of physics — you won't have time because action beats reaction.

This discussion has not even touched on the fact that every confrontation you may be in won't be a lethal force confrontation. Yet, if all you have is a lethal force option, your handgun, how will you defend yourself in less critical but nonetheless real confrontations and assaults?

We have been taught that lethal force attacks are to be countered with our lethal force option, our firearm. But too many people have been injured or killed by programming in that response exclusively. In the desperate, time-consuming attempt to get to their gun, they have presented a non-defending target to their attacker. *Rather than program ourselves to respond to a threat based on the severity of the threat, we should be training ourselves to respond based in the time available to us.* If when facing a lethal threat, we have time to seek cover and/or draw our firearm, great. If we don't, then we need to respond with our hands. The way we train for this reality is, as always, with realistic force-on-force scenarios, using firing, but non-lethal weapons such as Airsoft guns. If all of our firearms training consists of shooting at targets, then we aren't really training to engage in a fight, but simply honing our shooting skills.

In addition to firearm training, seek out hands-on defense skills such as weapon disarming, empty hands against a knife, martial

Because Airsoft training guns are such close replicas, it is a good idea to mark them with colored electrical tape on both the slides and grips so they can be identified as dummy guns when in your hand and in the holster.

arts, and other combative techniques, because it's a hand fight that you will most likely be in! If you don't practice in simulated full-speed, full-force fights, you will never acquire the skills you need to prevail in one.

Nine   GUN
SAFETY

Guns are not unsafe — they are just inanimate objects. However, people who use guns can be unsafe.

Before we can discuss gun usage, we need to delve into safety rules. Actually, these are mandates, not rules. Rules are made to be broken, mandates are not.

Treat every gun as if it is loaded

Some people like to bend safety rules when handling so-called 'unloaded' guns. The problem is that it develops bad habits. If you get into the habit of pointing an unloaded gun in an unsafe direction, you will one day find yourself pointing a loaded gun in an unsafe direction.

The biggest issue in ignoring this mandate is that you may be mistaken with regards to the gun's status. All too often someone has picked up a gun that was thought be unloaded, only to find a bullet in the chamber. Some people have also discovered it the hard way. Recently, a local police officer was indicted for murder when during a training exercise, the officer, a SWAT team sniper, aimed what he thought was an unloaded rifle at a police officer playing the role of a kidnapper. Having assumed that it was unloaded, he fired. Unfortunately, it wasn't and he was a good shot.[8]

Don't make the mistake of thinking that a gun is unloaded or won't fire just because the magazine is removed. Check the chamber! Treat all guns as if they are loaded!

Always point the gun in a safe direction

The definition of a safe direction changes depending on your location. No matter where you are, never point a gun at a person unless you intend on shooting that person. Likewise, never point a gun at any object unless you intend on destroying it. On the range, a safe direction is pointing at the backstop. In the home, safe is usually pointing downwards or upwards, unless there are people on the floor below or above you. If you are sandwiched between populated floors, then neither is a safe direction. The 'safer' direction would be towards an exterior wall, but keep in mind that bullets can go through walls, and that you are ultimately responsible for where your bullets go. If you haven't verified that a given direction is safe, then it isn't.

Keep guns unloaded

There is no reason for any gun to be loaded unless it is being carried in a holster for personal protection, stored properly for personal protection in the home or office, or at a range about to be fired. When out in plain sight, all guns should have their action open — revolvers should have the cylinder swung out (or the gun broken open and the rear of the cylinder visible in the case of old-fashioned "top break" revolvers), and semi-autos should have the slide locked back. If the slide doesn't lock, a pencil or similar object inserted in the ejection port will work. Doing this keeps the gun in a condition where it cannot be fired, and is easy to see that it is unloaded.

When picking up a gun, always check to see it is loaded — even if you 'know' that it is unloaded.

To check a revolver, simply swing out the cylinder.

Cycle the auto's slide back and look into the chamber. As a second check, place your pinky into the chamber to be sure it empty.

Keep your finger off the trigger until you are ready to shoot

Your finger should remain high on the side of the slide or cylinder at all times until you are actually ready to fire. During a draw, especially a fast draw, it is very easy to inadvertently place your finger in the trigger guard, or even on the trigger itself. This is extremely dangerous because it can easy cause an accidental discharge ("AD"). If that happens during a draw, there is a good chance that the

Trigger finger must remain on the frame or cylinder until ready to shoot.

shooter or a bystander may get hit with a bullet or ricochet.

If you are moving while your finger is in the trigger guard, a misstep or slip can cause an AD. If you are startled and jump from a loud noise, you can have an AD. If you simply are not cognizant of the pressure being placed on the trigger, an AD can occur.

Manual Safeties

Do not rely on a manual safety to make a gun safe. They should be considered only an additional step in your safety routine. The use of a manual safety does not allow you to point a gun somewhere you shouldn't, and may not even make the gun safe if it is dropped. Some safeties block the firing pin from moving forward to contact the primer, but many, especially some older designs, only block the trigger and/or hammer. If dropped, the inertia may be strong enough to send the firing pin into the primer, causing a discharge.

Know what you are shooting at

Bullets from a handgun can travel for many hundreds of feet. Know your target, what it is made of, and whether or not bullets will ricochet off or penetrate through it. Never shoot at a target that does not have a safe backstop behind it. It is important to be sure that your backstop will actually stop your bullets, and that the backstop is tall enough so that your shot does not go over it if you shoot above your intended target. On the range, shoot your handgun at reasonable handgun distances — bullets fired from a small-caliber handgun can drop to the ground and ricochet over a backstop.

On the street, all this changes. If you hit your intended target, the bullet may fully penetrate the body and hit someone else. In addition to paying attention to the person who intends you mortal harm, you also need to be concerned about bystanders, and what is behind the criminal. When the chips hit the fan, you **must** be aware of what you are firing at, what is nearby, and what is behind. If it is unsafe to shoot, **don't**. If you are uncertain, **don't**.

A miss might be safe on the range but is not safe on the street. When practicing, shoot slow enough to learn to hit what you shoot at. If you miss your target on the street, the bullet still goes somewhere. Think of a dead bystander every time you miss during practice as motivation to learn to shoot better.

Use the right ammunition

Make sure you are using the right caliber ammunition for your gun, and that it is of good quality. It can be very easy to mix up ammunition if you are shooting different calibers in different guns, especially if you are shooting them during the same session. A round that is too large could jam and fire unexpectantly, possibly before the slide is fully closed. Such a "slam fire" can damage both the gun and the shooter. A round that is too small could rotate, jam in the barrel, and again destroy the gun and your hand with it. Many different calibers of guns have been made over the past many years, and it is sometimes possible to find other calibers of ammunition that "sort of" fit your gun. Don't do it. Be smart — use only the caliber of ammunition that your gun's manufacturer designates.

Make sure your gun can handle the particular type of ammunition, as well. **Never** put Plus P (+P), Plus P Plus (+P+), or magnum ammunition in a gun not rated for it. If unsure, call the manufacturer for recommendations. Be especially careful of the lightweight guns as they often have ammunition restrictions.

Eye and ear protection

Wearing proper eye and ear protection is essential for all shooters and anyone in the surrounding area. Ricochet and splatter can hit anywhere. Casings from semi-auto guns fly out of the gun and can cut or burn.

Prolonged exposure or even a single gunshot can inflict permanent hearing damage.

Be sure to use quality eye and ear protection that was designed for firearm usage. Drugstore glasses and cotton balls just won't do.

Eye and ear protection is a must for shooters and observers.

Keep it clean

To keep your gun shooting safety and operating correctly, follow manufacturer's instructions to keep it properly clean and lubricated. Dirt and gunpowder residue between the slide and frame can keep the gun from cycling properly. A barrel fouled with lead residue, dirt, or even excess oil could bind the bullet and cause a blowout.

Alcohol and drugs don't mix with guns

If you are under the influence of any substance, including prescription drugs or over the counter medicine, do not pick up a gun. Alcohol and drugs lower reaction time and decrease mental capacity — not a good mix with firearms.

Range safety

If the range is monitored, obey the range officer immediately at all times. "Cease fire" does not mean stop shooting when you feel like it--it means stop shooting immediatly. If the range is "open", meaning that is does not have an official safety/range officer, you then are the range officer. Before shooting, make sure that all other shooters on the range are behind the firing line, have eye and ear protection, and give you permission to shoot.

Keep in mind your muzzle direction as you walk back and forth during your shooting. Unless you make a conscious effort, when you turn your body, the gun will turn with you. If you turn to talk to your neighbor, keep the gun aimed down range. Be extra cautious here as it is very easy to point a gun in an unsafe direction when moving.

Never carry a loaded gun as you walk back and forth from the target. Some ranges require all guns to be kept on the shooting bench with actions open. Otherwise, keep it in a holster. In either case, keep it unloaded.

On the range, keep the guns' actions open when not in use.

Do not touch your gun unless you are at the firing line, ready to fire. **Never** load your gun while behind the line. Even better, don't even touch your firearm when you are behind the line, so mistakes can't happen.

Never go downrange while loaded firearms are on, or behind the firing line.

If there is any question as to whether or not the firearm is working properly, stop shooting immediately and consult a gunsmith.

When you hand a firearm to someone else or when you place it down, do so with it unloaded, with the action open.

Never leave a gun unattended.

Never lean a loaded gun against anything.

Never handle a firearm or ammunition that you are unfamiliar with.

Clearing Jams

Don't look down the barrel to see what the problem is because you will be pointing the weapon at your face. Don't use a hard object like a screwdriver to pry or push. Use common sense. If you're not sure how to unjam or repair your gun, take it to a gunsmith.

GUN HANDLING BEYOND THE BASICS

Ten

The mandates of gun safety are vital, but to be completely safe, our gun handling skills must go beyond just the basics.

Probably one of the most dangerous and common gun handling mistakes is 'lasering', also known as 'crossing' or 'sweeping'. Many shooters seem to forget that bullets have a very long reach, and that everyone who is placed in front of a muzzle is placed in mortal danger. The term 'lasering' illustrates the concept that we can visualize a powerful laser that destroys anything that is in front of it, at any distance — in reality, not unlike a firearm. Take special care not to point the gun at yourself or others. When walking around on the range, or back and forth to the shooting line, always make sure that the muzzle is pointed in a safe direction, downrange.

Be extremely careful not to laser yourself during gun handling.

Manipulation of a firearm's action is an area where unsafe movements and lasering are all too common. Many people like to turn a gun sideways to work the action, but this potentially points the gun in an unsafe direction. When racking the slide or opening the cylinder, it is important to pay close attention to both your movements and the movements of the gun. Don't have your body remain stationary and then rotate the gun in a dangerous direction. Instead, turn your body, in relation to the gun, to keep the muzzle pointed

Never turn your gun sideways to rack the slide because it may point the gun at someone else.

safely down range.

Lasering is not just an issue for bystanders, but is also a major concern for shooters themselves. When drawing a gun, or reholstering, never point the muzzle inwards toward your body. If you can't get the gun into the holster without wiggling it back and forth, or using your other hand to hold

The proper way is to turn your body to keep the gun pointed safely downrange.

it open, that's a sure sign that you **need** a better quality holster.

While everyone knows the rule about treating all guns as if they are loaded, people consistently laser themselves and others with the muzzles of their 'unloaded' guns. It seems that people feel that if the gun is unloaded, they no longer need to be concerned about where it is pointing. There are two vital reasons why the 'All Guns Are Loaded' rule is important. 1. The assumption that 'it is unloaded' may be mistaken. 2. If we **always** treat a gun as if it is loaded, you will permanently imprint proper handling techniques in your mind, and will not mistakenly handle a loaded gun improperly. An astounding number of gun accidents happen with "unloaded" firearms.

The drawing of a firearm is potentially one of the most dangerous areas of gun handling. Make sure that your support hand follows or parallels the gun during the draw and does not get ahead of the muzzle. Make sure you don't laser your legs or feet as your bring the gun forward.

Do not release the external safety (if your gun has one) until you are on target and ready to fire. And **never** place your finger in the trigger guard unless you are prepared to destroy whatever the gun is pointing at.

Many, many accidental discharges happen during reholstering because the trigger finger is left in the trigger guard. Every instant that you are not firing your weapon, your trigger finger **must** be high against your slide or cylinder.

When you have finished shooting on the range, lock back the slide on autos, and open the cylinder on revolvers. Keep them that way until you are ready to shoot again. This allows you, and everyone else, to see that the gun is empty. If you hand your gun to someone else, give it to them open.

When checking to see if an auto is loaded, some people use the 'pinch test' technique, which I find scary. The 'pinch' entails gripping the slide from underneath just behind the muzzle and pulling the slide back slightly in order to see if it's loaded. If an accidental discharge happens, I don't want my fingers that close to the muzzle. If you need to rack the slide, get into the habit of griping it from the rear of the pistol.

The 'pinch test' is not a good idea because it puts the fingers too close to the muzzle.

When unloading, be sure to remove the magazine first, then rack the slide to clear the chamber. Doing it in the reverse order leaves a round in the chamber. When you shoot to slide lock, don't assume the gun is empty. Always check, because an auto could also slide lock through vibration or because of a mechanical problem, leaving you with a live round still in the gun.

Just because the safety is 'on' does not make the gun safe. See Mandate 1.

When racking the slide to unload, the first instinct for many people is to grab the slide from the top with the entire hand, but that is very unsafe. While it may offer a strong grip, it is inherently dangerous because your flesh covers the ejection port. Open the slide of an semi-auto and look inside towards the back. Does the

In the event of a malfunction do **not** cover the ejection port with your hand during clearing. Cycle the slide from the rear for safety.

ejector have a resemblance to a firing pin? Many people have learned the hard way that when a live round is dislodged, the primer can get pushed back against the ejector. The resulting detonation will destroy the flesh that covers the ejection port. Resist the temptation for a stronger grip, and keep your hand and face far away from the ejection port while unloading or clearing a jam.

Whenever you practice with gun, a new holster, or a new technique, always start at a slow and safe speed. Increase the tempo in steps only when competence and muscle memory is achieved.

With familiarity comes complacency. The more we train with our firearms, the more we owe it to ourselves to be extra cautious. If you see someone on the range demonstrating unsafe gun handling skills, approach them politely and explain how they can conduct themselves in a safer manner. The life you save may be your own.

Eleven # TRIGGER SYSTEMS

Both revolvers and semi-autos can have either a single or a double action trigger. A single action trigger design means that the pull of the trigger does only one thing — release the hammer (or striker) to fire the gun. The single action trigger has a relatively

short, light pull. This design is used on 1911 style and other semi-automatic pistols, and some revolvers. Double action revolvers become single action when the hammer is manually pulled back until it locks.

A double action trigger, as the name implies, does two things: cocks the hammer (or striker), then

Les Baer 1911 with single action trigger

releases the hammer or striker to fire the gun. With a typical semi-automatic pistol, the slide cocks the hammer when it is pulled back for loading, and then again after each round fires. The trigger on a double action revolver also pulls the hammer back, and then releases it.

A trigger that works only in double action mode is known as a 'double action only', or 'DAO.' A relatively new variant, the double/single trigger, offers a double action pull on the first shot with the trigger being set into the single action mode after firing the first shot. Double/single triggers, are known as 'double action'('DA').

Taurus' DAO Millennium

A single action trigger usually has a light trigger pull of 3 to 5 pounds and a short pull length of only 1/8 inch or so. A double action trigger typically requires 5-12 lbs. of pressure with a half inch or so of travel.

It is true that the single action trigger design is the more accurate trigger design because of its light and short trigger pull. While a trigger system does not directly affect the accuracy of a firearm, the manipulation of the trigger by the user does. The less pressure that needs to be applied over the shortest distance, the less the gun will be negatively affected by the shooter pressing the trigger. A double action trigger with a heavy, long pull cannot be shot as fast and as accurately as a single action trigger by most shooters. I say by most shooters, because there are top shooters that can shoot double action pistols very fast and very accurately. That level of proficiency is only possible with lots of practice.

While I say that a gun with a double action trigger is less accurate than one with a single action trigger, let me elaborate on why I don't mind having a 'less accurate' gun to defend my life with. Simply put, while less accurate, it is only *slightly* less accurate, and the gun is more than accurate enough at combat distances, and beyond.

Most gunfights happen at less than 10 feet — some say at less than 7 feet. Even out to 30 to 40 feet, a double action gun can certainly be fired accurately enough if the shooter trains with it. If a skilled shooter can shoot 2-inch groups at 30 feet with a single action firearm, the switch to a double action gun may open the group size to 4 inches. Even a 6-inch group would very acceptable. At 10 feet, the difference would hardly even be noticeable.

New Trigger Systems

In the last few years, a new fad of double/single action triggers has become inexplicably popular. I say inexplicably, because I consider it to be a solution to a problem that does not exist. Many top name manufacturers not only make double/single guns, but the design often dominates their product line. Personally, I don't understand why.

The double/single trigger has a decocking mechanism that lowers the hammer after loading, so that the first shot is in double action mode. As the slide moves back after discharge, the hammer remains cocked and the trigger then acts as a single action on future shots. The main problem with this design is that if you are choosing a double action trigger to reduce the possibility of an AD, (why else would you choose a double action?) the advantage is mooted by the change to single action after the first shot. Some have suggested that the first shot is all you need the double action trigger for since after you start shooting, you have no need to be concerned. I totally disagree. After you have taken down your first attacker, you still need to keep your weapon safe as you search for, or engage, other attackers as well as deal with victims, bystanders, and witnesses. In my mind, it is never safe to have a single action trigger when your heart is pumping a mile a minute, you have impaired mental capacity, limited vision, reduced hearing, and you can't feel your fingers.

If that weren't reason enough, I find the change from a long hard trigger pull to a short light pull to be disconcerting. For me, I find it easier to shoot when the trigger pull is consistent from shot to shot. The industry may have realized these issues as recently more and more guns are coming to market with a DAO design.

Before you run out and buy a gun with a double action trigger, shop around, as not all double action triggers are created equal. Some have longer trigger reaches than others, some have heavier pulls than others, and some have smoother triggers than others. The triggers on striker-fired guns feel completely different than triggers on hammer-fired guns.

The Para-Ordinance LDA and striker-fired guns like the Glocks, Kahrs, and Springfield Armory XDs (and others) have added new words to the gun vernacular. Rather than hitting a firing pin with a hammer as a traditional trigger system does, the triggers of a striker fired pistol release an internal spring-loaded striker. With double action strikers, the trigger first sets the striker back, then releases it. With single action strikers, the slide motion sets the striker back, and the trigger releases it.

Springfield Armory's XD

The single action striker pistol defies easy categorization, as it defies the meaning of both single and double action trigger systems. In most cases, double action denotes a long hard trigger pull and single action denotes a short light pull. In the case of the single action striker, the trigger pull is approximately the same length and weight of the double action striker trigger even though it performs only a single action. As an example the trigger of the single action XD feels and acts very much like the trigger of the double action striker Glock.

The LDA by Para Ordinance is

Para Ordinance LDA

a *light* double action with a long pull, meaning the hammer spring is partially cocked internally by the action of the slide, but the hammer remains forward. Since the spring is already tensioned, the trigger pull required to move the hammer down and fire the gun is 'light'.

Personally, I prefer a medium weight trigger, with a short to medium pull length with an action that is as smooth as possible. Having small hands, the larger guns with long trigger reaches don't work for me. I prefer a medium weight trigger rather than heavy because it still does the job of making the trigger more noticeable to my finger while under stress, but does not over do it and throw off my shots.

Twelve

ARE SINGLE ACTION TRIGGERS STREET SAFE?

As discussed in the previous chapter, the single action trigger design offers a light, short trigger pull. It is the most accurate and easiest to shoot trigger system because the less motion that is required to actuate the trigger, the less the movement of the trigger finger will negatively effect the aim of the gun. A light, short pull is the single action trigger's greatest asset, but it can also be its greatest detriment.

I own several 1911 handguns with single action triggers. They are one of my favorite gun designs and I carried one for nearly ten years. I love their light, short triggers, and they feel great in my hand. But after an accidental discharge at a competition and some subsequent research, I now feel that firearms with single action triggers are unsafe for defense use in all but the most highly trained hands, including mine. (In this case, 'highly trained' means lots of training under the most realistic and highly stressful, real-life situations possible.) My conclusion is based on the body's subconscious reactions to high levels of stress, such as those created by a lethal encounter.

The reason that there has been a dramatic shift to double action and double action only trigger systems by the law enforcement community and armed citizens alike is that the longer and heavier pull of double action triggers is more noticeable to the user and therefore it is less likely that the trigger will be actuated accidentally. Many pistoleros reject that theory claiming that single action triggers are perfectly safe if the operator just keeps his finger off the trigger. Based on my observations, experience, and research that is not the simple answer that it seems. The stress of a lethal encounter will cause many physiological changes in your body and brain, which may have potentially negative effects on your ability to use your firearm safely.

All the practice in the world on a basic shooting range will not completely prepare you for the stress effects of an actual real-life lethal encounter. Under the severe levels of stress, your body may react with a startle response and Body Alarm Reaction (BAR) will take over. BAR symptoms include: tunnel vision, auditory exclusion, and loss of minute motion control of appendages such as fingers, and time distortion. (See Chapter 5 for more information on

"Body Alarm Reaction")

Tunnel vision causes your eyes/brain to concentrate on the threat. In a life or death struggle, you many see only your attacker, only the hands of your attacker, or possibly only the weapon. You may never even see additional attackers, bystanders, or the backstop of your potential shot.

Auditory exclusion will drastically limit your hearing. You may hear just muffled sounds or just hear the voice of your attacker. Many people report never even hearing the sound of their own gun fire.

Blood restrictions will limit your body's fine motor control, and will also reduce the communication that lets your brain know that your body parts are moving or even that they have come in contact with an object, such as a trigger. A racing heartbeat can make your body and hands shake.

Your sense of time can be greatly exaggerated. You may feel that you are moving in slow motion. Ten seconds may seem like minutes.

Your initial startle response alone may be enough to cause a restriction of your muscles and cause your firearm to accidentally discharge. Humans are born with a startle response as part of our survival instincts. While everyone experiences different levels of startle response, some effects can be expected. Have you ever jumped when you came across someone that you did not expect while rounding a corner? That's one example of a startle response.

Here's an interesting demonstration to see the effect of clenching your hand muscle in similar fashion to what a startle may produce; hold your shooting hand out straight with the palm vertical, curl your bottom three finger and extend your trigger finger as if you were gripping a gun. Clench your fist a few times. Does your trigger finger move when you clench the rest of your fingers? What might happen if you were startled while holding a gun with your finger on, or near, the trigger?

These issues did not really sink in until I had an accidental discharge at an IPSC match. During a particularly stressful, fast reload my finger pressed the trigger without me being aware of it until the round fired. It is commonly stated that ADs are caused by poor gun handling skills and you just need to train yourself to keep your finger off the trigger. Well, I practiced keeping my finger off the trigger for 20 years. The difference at the match was that the higher level of stress that I was experiencing for the first time affected my abilities and awareness.

A few weeks after my AD, I did a training session on a FATS system, (Fire Arm Training Simulation), which uses real handguns converted to shoot lasers at a movie screen displaying simulated tactical scenarios. With the remembrance of my AD fresh in my mind, I specifically checked my finger during and after stressful encounters. I found my finger subconsciously on the trigger three times during the one-hour session! This proved to me that even twenty years of shooting a 1911 and several seasons of action shooting competitions did not prepare me for the effects that higher levels of stress cause.

Firearm Training System (FATS) utilizes real guns converted to fire lasers at an interactive screen.

Coincidentally, a short time later, I came across details of a law enforcement test that demonstrated that under high levels of stress, the trigger finger often **subconsciously** travels to the trigger to 'confirm its position'. Lt. Dave Spaulding, of the Montgomery County, Ohio Sheriffs Office, observed that 632 out of 674 officers tested periodically placed their fingers in the trigger guard during FATS training. This is astounding — 94% of the trained police officers tested placed their finger on the trigger under stress! This number included many highly skilled and motivated officers. The officers that he observed doing these "trigger searches" had no memory of doing so.[9]

Lt. Spaulding's research confirms that high levels of stress affect the shooter's subconscious actions. While I, and those officers, trained to keep our fingers off the trigger, the effects of stress caused the **unconscious** movement of the trigger finger, thus creating a very dangerous situation.

An accidental discharge is more likely with a single action trigger than a double action trigger because of its short, light trigger pull. Had I been using a single action trigger during my FATS exercise, I might have had three ADs, because all it takes to fire a single action gun is just a relatively light touch of the trigger. What probably prevented an AD in the FATS training session was that the laser weapon had a double action trigger, which was not set off by my slight touch.

My conclusion is that unless you train extensively under extreme stress, the double action trigger would be a safer choice for defense. While the double action trigger is safer than a single action trigger because of the heavier weight and longer pull of the trigger, it is not the total solution. You still need to train to keep your finger off the trigger until you are ready to destroy what your gun is pointing at.

Thirteen # REVOLVERS VS. SEMI-AUTOMATICS

I always recommend revolvers to new shooters, and very often to seasoned shooters as well. While they may not have the machismo of an semi-automatic, revolvers offer many advantages not found elsewhere.

Revolvers are the archetype of simplicity — load, point, pull trigger. Revolvers are very intuitive. Anyone can just pick one up and use it. Except for minor differences in the operation of the cylinder catch, all double action revolvers work the same way. If you know how to use one revolver, you know how to use them all. In a gunfight, if you need to give someone your backup revolver to assist you, they will instantly know how to use it without looking for, or fumbling with, the safeties, decockers, and slide stops that are found on semi-automatics.

Revolvers symbolize the ultimate in reliability. With so few moving parts, breakage is far less of an issue compared to autos.

Jams are practically a non-issue with revolvers. Reliability issues with semi-autos include failure to feed, failure to eject, double feed, etc. Some problems are equipment related, many are ammunition related. Ammunition choice will make or break an auto. Many, dare I say most, autos are ammunition sensitive. Some rounds they like, some they don't. All autos require ammunition reliability tests. Before I will carry it or use it for home defense, a semi-automatic must fire at least 200 rounds of my carry ammunition without any type of failure whatsoever. If not, it goes to the gunsmith, and the test starts over again. In fact, some manufacturers require shooting a couple hundred rounds as part of the break-in procedure. With the high cost of quality carry ammunition, expect to spend $120 to $150 for every 200-round ammunition test for an auto. You can buy a good revolver for the cost of a couple semi-auto ammunition tests alone.

Revolvers are not ammunition sensitive. With quality factory ammunition, a revolver will go bang every time, no matter what the bullet design, shape or size. In the rare instance that an ammunition-related failure does occur in a revolver, there is no need for a complicated clearance drill. Simply pull the trigger again. Not having to do extensive ammunition tests saves time, and especially money. One note: if an ammunition failure in a revolver causes the round to lodge itself against the frame, it may take a gunsmith to repair it. Fortunately, with quality ammunition from top manufacturers, this type of ammunition failure is highly unlikely.

Normal residue from gunpowder and lead can jam an auto loader. Many autos require cleaning after a few hundred rounds in order to keep functioning properly. Dust, dirt, and mud (if the gun is dropped) can work their way between the frame and slide to hinder an auto's functioning. Maintenance, while still necessary, is much less of an issue with a revolver. The fewer moving parts and the greater tolerances between the parts of a revolver help keep it functioning when dirty. While the powder probably won't jam a revolver, it may make the rounds hard to insert and eject. Cleaning every time you shoot or between every few hundred rounds should keep it functioning smoothly.

Hammer with spur.

Spurless hammer.

Revolvers make great pocket guns because they do not have reciprocating slides, their shape (with a spurless or internal hammer) allows a smooth draw with nothing to catch on the clothing, and they are not very sensitive to pocket lint. A concealed hammer revolver can even be fired unfettered while in a pocket, because the fully enclosed hammer has nothing to catch on or obstruct its movement. There is no faster draw than firing a gun that is still in your pocket! While many autos are small enough

Internal hammer.

Firing through your pocket is the ultimate surprise defense.

to fit in a pocket, the shape of the slide often hinders the draw. If you fire while in your pocket, you can't get more than one shot off without the gun jamming, because the slide will bind against the cloth and/or your body. A pocket auto needs constant cleaning to keep the pocket lint from causing a malfunction, even with the use of a pocket holster.

Revolvers offer a fist full of power in a small package. Popular calibers such as .38 Special, and my favorite, .357 Magnum, are available in small J-frame-sized guns that are great for both daily carry and home use. With the exception of a few models, most autos in that size don't offer nearly that much punch.

Revolvers are plentiful on the used market offering great values. Even new, many revolvers sell for half of what the average quality autoloader costs.

Loading and unloading a revolver is simple, quick, and can even be done easily in the dark. To check if it's loaded, just open the cylinder and feel if the rounds are where they are supposed to be. In the light, you just have to look. While you can easily load a semi-auto in the dark, it is very difficult to check if it is loaded properly without light, as only a small percentage of semi-autos feature an external loaded chamber indicator. Even with the lights on, you need to first check the auto's chamber and then remove the magazine to check it as well.

Handling and using a revolver is safer than a single action auto because you don't have to worry about extremely light triggers or forgetting to drop the safety or having the slide stop hang. Accidental discharges happen because someone places their finger on the trigger before they are ready to shoot. While this can certainly happen with a revolver, it happens less often because of the longer and heavier trigger pull. (Double action autos also have this benefit). The revolver trigger is more forgiving than most autos but you still need to be careful.

If you are like most people, you have on at least one occasion, forgotten to release the safety on your auto. That's not a good idea when your life depends on your getting off a shot. Revolvers have no manual safeties to forget. (Some double action autos also do not have manual safeties).

One issue that is often overlooked, especially with new shooters, is 'limp wristing'. If the gun is held loosely in the hand, a semi-auto's slide may not have enough to pressure to push against in order to cycle properly, thus jamming the gun. Limp wristing tends to happen to new shooters who might be afraid of the gun, or to anyone who fires while not having a proper, solid grip. This could include you if you had already been attacked and were shaking from adrenaline or, even worse, were weak from blood loss. With no reciprocating slide, revolvers will fire regardless of the grip.

With all the advantages of a revolver and all of the problems with an auto loader, why would anyone carry an auto? Firepower, speed and accuracy are the benefits; however, as we can see, there is a price to pay for them.

Most revolvers are 5 or 6-shooters. While this is plenty for most situations, logical and reasonable arguments can be made for larger capacity firearms. Most autos usually have at least 6 rounds and many go to 18 rounds, depending of the caliber and size of the gun.

Autos tend to be faster and more accurate in well-trained hands than revolvers because of the shorter and lighter triggers that many models offer. Autos are faster to reload.

Here's what I suggest to people regarding autos. You should only carry an auto if you are willing to:

- Ammunition test it with at least 200 rounds of the ammunition that you are going to carry. And every time a repair or adjustment is made that could affect feeding, ammunition test it again. Autos are too ammunition sensitive not to be sure that everything is functioning perfectly.

- Practice with it consistently to keep yourself extremely familiar with its functions and safeties. I'm talking about practicing every couple of months minimum, not just once a year. At least once a week you should practice dry firing, including drawing and dropping the safety (if there is one). Practice keeping your trigger finger high along the slide/ frame to keep from having an AD. Practice keeping your finger off the trigger until you are ready to fire. Remember to keep safety in mind while you dry fire, always keeping the muzzle pointed in a safe direction.

- Clean it religiously every time you shoot to keep it functioning.

- Learn how to overcome failures to feed, failures to eject, and double feeds and practice clearing them. Even the most reliable auto loaders can have occasional jams. If it puts your pistol out of service at the wrong time, you could be in deep trouble — 6 feet deep.

- Practice loading, reloading, and unloading, both in the dark and in the light.

If you are dedicated enough in your training and discipline, an auto may have a place in your holster. But for many, the revolver offers the perfect combination of ease-of-use and functionality.

Fourteen

CLEARING JAMS
AND MALFUCNTIONS

If it moves, it can jam. Jams and malfunctions are, unfortunately, a fact of life with semi-automatics. In the event of a problem, it is imperative to understand what caused the issue, because that will directly effect what type of correction needs to be made. Assuming no operator errors and assuming that you are using a properly functioning gun that feeds properly, (if not, see a gunsmith or send it back to the manufacturer) there are five main malfunctions that you may encounter; failure to fire, failure to eject, double feed, failure to go into battery, and squibs.

Murphy's law is alive and well and you should expect and be prepared for a problem at the worst time. The best solution for a malfunction during a gun fight may be to switch to a back-up gun — but that may not be an available or practical alternative. Either way, it is important to learn what can cause a particular jam or malfunction and practice identifying the problem and correcting it so if it happens at a particularly sensitive moment, you will instinctively know what do to. As hard as it might be to imagine, a proper training regiment includes making your gun fail…and practice fixing it.

The first thing to do with all problems is to get fully behind cover, otherwise you will be out in the open, fully exposed and preoccupied. I remind you of this even though you should already be behind cover! Don't forget: a jammed gun is still a loaded gun. Keep the muzzle pointed in a safe directions and follow all gun safety mandates.

Failure to Fire

If you hear a 'click' rather than a 'bang' you have experienced what is known as a 'failure to fire'. In a gunfight, a 'click' is the loudest noise you will ever hear! Very commonly, 'failure to fire' is due to a misfeed caused by the magazine not being seated properly within the gun during loading. Assuming that you actually did pull back the slide to load the gun, the solution is the classic 'tap and rack'. Tap the magazine in (hard) with the butt of your hand and rack the slide to feed a new round. If you were reloading the gun with a live round in the chamber, the 'tap and rack' will eject the chambered round and will strip a new one from the magazine. The 'tap and rack' is a good technique to try just about any time there is a failure.

To "tap and rack", reseat the magazine by a stern hit
with the hand and a rack of the slide.

Another potential cause of failure to fires could be a weak
magazine spring. If feeding issues happen often with the same
magazine, it is probably the magazine spring or other damage to
the magazine — look for dents and compare the magazine opening
to another to see if the lips have been compressed or damaged in
any way. If feeding problems persist with several magazines you
probably are not inserting the magazine into the gun firmly enough.
Some high capacity magazines, if filled to the limit, exert excessive
pressure against the cartridge making the magazine difficult to seat
properly. If this is the case, simply load one less round than full
capacity.

TIP: Label your magazines with paint underneath the basepad
to help identify your magazine easily. I use numbers for my
practice/competition magazines and I use letters to identify my
carry magazines.

If the magazine is not at fault, it could be an issue with the
firing system; either a weak/broken hammer spring or broken firing
pin. To diagnose these issues check the primer hit. Compare the
depth of the primer hit to other spent cases. If there is no dimple,
you probably have a broken firing pin. If it's a shallow hit, you
have either a broken or weak spring or a broken firing pin. See a
gunsmith for advice.

If it's not the magazine and not the firing system, it could be
bad ammunition. Change ammunition and try the rounds you are
having a problem with in another gun to see if it also misfires.

A good way to practice clearing drills is to place a dummy
round mixed in with your bullets. The best method to do this
is to have a friend load your magazines for you and place a few
dummies intermixed in *some* of your magazines so you don't know
which magazines have them and which do not, nor will you know
when to expect them in the magazines that do. Treat the "failure"

in training as you would in real life — Get fully behind cover, diagnose, repair, reload.

Failure to Eject

Ejection problems can stem from many causes. If the extractor is weak or broken the casing will not be extracted from the chamber properly. A 'stove pipe' occurs if the casing only partially ejects and gets caught in the slide. The solution is to simply brush your hand firmly along the top of the slide in a 'karate chop' method to dislodge the casing or run the 'tap and rack' drill turning the gun sideways to help the ejection. Casings could occasionally stove pipe but if the problem persists it could be a bad ejector or the main recoil spring could be too heavy, thus interfering with the slide motion. If your recoil spring is factory spec have a smith check the extractor and ejector. If you are using reloads a weak charge could also be the culprit.

Stove pipe.

'Karate chop' along the slide to clear a stove pipe malfunction.

Double Feed

A double feed occurs when the previous round or casing does not eject and the slide picks up a new round from the magazine jamming it against the one still in the chamber. The double feed is considered to be the most serious of the jams because it is the most time consuming to clear — so much so that in a gun fight the gun should considered useless and your backup weapon should be employed.

In order to clear a double

Double feed.

feed you need to drop your magazine, empty the chamber and reload. The magazine will be lodged firmly in the gun, held in by the round it is trying to feed. To release it, you first need to lock back the slide to relieve pressure, press the magazine release button and pull the magazine from the gun. Mostly likely the magazine will be held tight and some force will be needed. To eject the original round, rack the slide firmly a few times. If that does not dislodge it, you will need to lock back the slide and slip a pencil or similar object through the barrel to push the round/casing out. Once the round is ejected, insert a new magazine (since the old one may have contributed to the problem or may have been damaged), rack the slide, and you are ready to fire.

Failure To Go In To Battery

If a round does not completely seat in the chamber it is known as a 'failure to go into battery". These types of failures can be

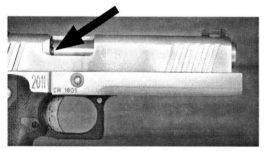

A failure to go into battery can be recognized by the slide not cycling completely. Note the open chamber (arrow) and the nose of the slide is not flush with the frame.

Casing may be visible in the chamber opening with a failure to go into battery malfunction (arrow).

Hit the back of the slide to push it forward.

caused by a gun that is dirty or a by a round that bulges. A dirty gun can slow the slide motion reducing its ability to push the round completely into the chamber and fouling can reduce the chamber's width, keeping the round from completely seating. Bulging rounds are commonly found in reloads and are caused by the resizing die not being completely cycled downward. With either situation, hit the back of the slide with the bony part of the bottom of your open palm. If the slide does not then fully engage, you will need to lock open your slide, drop the magazine and run a pencil or similar object down the barrel to dislodge it.

Squibs

A squib is a round that lodges in the barrel because the cartridge did not have enough, or any, gunpowder. This is a common error with hand-made reloads. The first sign that you have a squib load is when you hear a 'pop' instead of a 'bang'. The pop is the sound of the primer exploding in an empty case. If you hear a 'pop', **stop shooting immediately**. If you continue shooting with a bullet blocking the barrel the gun will most likely explode.

To clear a squib, remove the magazine and lock back the slide. Insert a pencil-shaped object down the front of the barrel and push the bullet out. It should come out with not much effort.

Clearing Revolvers

With fewer moving parts than semi-autos and no feeding issues to be concerned with, revolvers jams tend to be really easy to fix or really difficult — with not much in the middle. The two most common jams with revolvers are 'squibs' and high primers.

A high primer is where the primer is not fully seated and protrudes slightly out the bottom of the round. This protrusion rubs against the frame of the gun and stiffens the rotation of the cylinder or jams it completely. To unjam, hold the cylinder locking mechanism open and swing out the cylinder. This may take significant pressure. Remember you have a live round in the gun — keep it pointed in safe direction at all times.

In a revolver, the squib round clears the same way as a semi-auto — open the cylinder and insert a pencil shaped object down the front of the barrel and push the bullet out.

These malfunctions are the common ones that can occur with any type and brand of firearm. Practice identifying problems and clearing jams as you would any other technique. With empty guns and dummy rounds. Learn the movements slowly and speed up with practice.

Not all jams can be cleared easily. If you can't unjam it yourself, it's safer to let a professional help — especially if it's a live round that's causing the problem. Carefully pack up the gun, and tell the gunsmith about the problem and the fact that your gun is loaded **before** you hand it over. Better yet, let the gunsmith unpack it.

Fifteen   HANDGUN SELECTION

Revolver or semi-automatic? Small, medium, or large frame? .22, .25, .32, .380, 9mm, .38 Special, .357 Magnum, .357 SIG, .41, .40 S&W, .44 Special, 44 Magnum or .45 ACP? With lots of choices of guns and calibers it can be confusing — especially so for the new shooter.

If you take just one tip from this chapter, here it is: Find a gun that you can shoot quickly and accurately and that you can carry comfortably. The gun won't do you any good if you can't hit what you are aiming at, or if you leave it home because it's too big and heavy.

Let's start with the basics for the first time gun owner. When asked which gun to buy for a new shooter, most experts highly recommend a revolver. Simply stated, a revolver is simple — idiot proof. Pull the trigger, it goes bang.

Semi-autos can be finicky. They need proper maintenance, need a good match of ammunition to make them reliable, require lots of practice to become competent in their use and they can, and often do, jam. With all that against them, why would anyone carry a semi-auto? A properly serviced, well-maintained semi-auto with the correct ammunition can offer a large number of rounds, can be reloaded faster, and can be shot faster than a revolver, if it is in the hands of an experienced, trained shooter.

Don't think you can just buy any gun, especially a semi-auto, stick some ammunition in it, and you are ready to protect your family. Just as trying to fly a plane without lessons is not advisable, knowledge, training, and practice are essential in the use of firearms.

Revolver Options

For the most part, revolvers come in four sizes. Mini guns, most often utilizing substandard calibers (less than 9mm) can be as small as a pack of cigarettes. Small revolvers such as the "J" frame size from Smith and Wesson and others hold 5 cartridges. Medium and large frame revolvers carry 6 rounds, and some newer models even carry 7 or 8 rounds. Many of the smaller guns offer models made of various exotic materials, which reduces their weight. The steel guns are heavier than the alloy ones and offer reduced recoil because of their heft. The alloy and other lightweight guns are easier to carry, but some people find the recoil too heavy because the low weight does little to reduce the muzzle lift. I own both ultra-light weight and stainless steel revolvers. Personally, I much prefer to carry the steel because I find it easier to control when firing, giving me better accuracy and faster follow up shots.

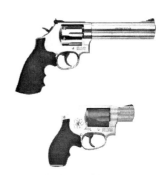

6-inch and 2-inch barreled revolvers.

The choice of size and weight of a gun should be determined as a matter of personal taste, based on what you can physically handle. Being a person of small stature, I prefer the small and medium frames, rather than large. I simply cannot properly reach the trigger on the large framed guns.

While on the subject of trigger reach, a proper placement of the trigger seats the trigger on, or just before, the first joint of your finger with a revolver or double action auto. With a single action gun, the trigger should be right in the middle of the pad of the finger for best trigger control.

When testing the size of the gun, I found out the hard way (and the expensive way) that the way you pick up a gun effects the way you hold it in your hand. Pick up the gun differently and it may give you a different impression on the fit of the gun. I find that if I pick a gun up off a table, my hand seems to slide slightly towards the trigger, which gives me a false perception of a shorter trigger reach. When I do a proper draw from a holster, I find that my hand does not similarly migrate improperly. Since from a holster is how I will use the gun, the trigger needs to fit me from a draw. While a local gun shop may not have a holster for you to try, do what you can to reproduce real-life carry circumstances while testing.

Place the double action trigger at the first joint.

Place the single action trigger on the pad of the finger.

By far, the best way to test the fit of a gun is to borrow one from a friend or someone at the gun range and use it. Nothing will teach you more about a gun than using it! If you buy a gun that does not fit your hand, you will not be able to shoot it as well as you could shoot one that does.

Besides the size and weight of the frame, barrel length needs to be considered as well. The longer the barrel, the faster the bullet travels, the better the stopping power, and the lower the recoil will be. However, the shorter barreled guns are easier to carry and draw. For a carry revolver, 1 to 3 inch barrels are easiest to draw. 4 to 5 inch barrels can be easily carried, but are a little more difficult to draw. If you are tall, the longer distance between your hand and your armpit will allow you to draw a longer length. For carry and home use, I like 3 to 4-inch revolvers.

Choosing an Auto

So you promise to learn about proper usage, find the right ammunition, clean it, and practice as discussed in the previous chapter and you are ready to move to a semi-auto? Most of the revolver advice holds true for a semi-auto, but with a few other considerations thrown in.

Many autos not only come in different barrel lengths, but different grip lengths also. The grip of a full-size gun offers comfortable placement for all 3 fingers (the trigger finger does not count because it does not wrap around the grip). The next size down allows a 2-finger grip or a tight 3-finger grip for those with small hands. Magazine extensions are sometimes available that can provide the same 3-fingered grip as on the larger sized gun. Other smaller models even have a 1-finger grip. Most people I know that carry, use a full-size or 2-finger grip. Even with my small hands, I find the full-size grip the most comfortable and controllable.

1 finger on Seecamp 32.
2 fingers on Keltec 3AT.
3 fingers on Sig 239.

One consideration of grip size is reload technique. The shorter 2, and 1-finger grips require that the pinky, and perhaps the middle finger, be only partially on the grip or underneath the grip. In both cases, the finger(s) needs to be moved in order to replace the magazine. If you don't move your finger when reloading, you could cause a severe pinch when the magazine traps your finger between itself and the grip. Ask me how I know.

Another obvious disadvantage is that the smaller grips hold less rounds, depending on the gun and the caliber. The only advantage to a smaller grip is that the butt of the gun doesn't stick out as far as the full size models when being carried. While this is a serious consideration for concealment, in most cases, a proper holster will allow most people to carry and conceal full size guns.

Barrel length does not affect concealability if you carry an 'in-the-waistband' (IWB) holster since the barrel is not visible. It does affect concealability if you carry on the belt. In either case, the barrel length does affect your ability to draw. The longer the barrel, the more you have to lift your gun in order to clear the holster. Practice with and test different barrel lengths in the type of holster you plan to use, to see what works best for you.

Unique to semi-autos, an additional decision needs to be made regarding capacity. Most autos hold between 6-10 rounds. Some models can accommodate double stack magazines that will hold up to 19 rounds, depending on caliber. **NOTE: Be aware that some jurisdictions prohibit magazines that hold more than ten rounds. Check your local laws.** For those guns where double stack magazines are available, the advantage is obvious — more bullets in the gun. The drawback is the extra weight and wider grip circumference which, depending on your size, may make it harder to hold and to conceal.

An 8-round single stack .45 and a 14-round double stack .45 magazine.

Your personal taste, physical stature, and size of pocketbook are all considerations in this decision.

Pointing

Thought we were done? Nope! Another very important element of proper gun choice for any gun is its pointing. I want a gun that **naturally** points properly. That means that the sights are lined up level without me having to angle my wrist up or down. There is only one way to accurately test the pointing — with your eyes closed! Hold an unloaded gun down at your side or in front of you. Close your eyes and aim the gun on a safe target. Open your eyes and check the sights. If the sights are lined up to each other (within reason), the gun points properly for you. Do it a few times. If you find the front sight consistently too high or too low, pick another gun.

Some people simply say that training will help you change the point of aim. While that is true, why train your body to do something unnatural when you don't have to? The same amount of training on a gun that points well will get you further in the long run.

Weight

In recent years, there has been a lot of attention paid to the weight of guns. Glock pioneered the use of lightweight polymer frames in early 80s. Lots of other manufacturers now offer polymer and metal alloy frames in light-weight versions of many of their popular models. The weight of a gun is a two-edged sword. On one hand, the lighter guns are easier to carry. On the other, the heavier guns are easier and faster to shoot because of the lighter recoil. If you can find ones to borrow, try them both and see how much the heavier weight really bothers you or if the increased recoil from the lighter gun is a problem.

I prefer the heavier guns because of the better shooting characteristics, and I don't mind carrying the extra heft. I went from an alloy gun to a steel framed one when I started carrying a longer barrel length. The weight difference wasn't that noticeable but the increased control was.

I also recently changed my pocket gun from an ultra-light weight .38 to a full steel .357. I changed in favor of the better stopping power of the .357, and because the extra heavy recoil of the light weight frame shifted the gun in my hand when shooting, resulting in slow follow-up shots due to the need to reposition and re-aim the gun after each shot fired.

Before I switched, I carried the steel .357 in my pocket for three days to see how long I could carry it before the weight bothered me. It surprised me to realize that I didn't even notice a difference with the heavier gun. As an experiment, I carried the ultra-light weight (12 oz., empty) in one pocket and the full steel (33 oz., empty) in the other. Again, no problem, even when carrying side by side. One difference is that with the ultra-light, I could keep my belt loose or even not wear one. With the heavier gun, I need to wear my belt slightly tightened because if it were loose, the weight would pull my belt down uncomfortably against my hipbone. I often carry the full steel .357 in my pocket fourteen hours a day without being bothered by its weight.

Gunsmithing and Modifications

While action competitors and target shooters may do a high level of customization to their guns, it is usually a very bad idea to modify guns used for personal defense because of safety and liability issues.

It is **very** important **not** to make any modifications to defense guns other than a 'double action only' trigger conversion, trigger action smoothing, and reliability work. If you are involved in an incident with a modified gun, the prosecutor could paint you as a hotshot, someone so anxious to shoot someone that you custom modified your gun to make it more deadly, or someone who took deliberate action that recklessly reduced the level of safety of their firearm. How do you think that would sound to the jury?

Revolvers can safely have the hammer spurs removed to convert to double action only and the trigger mechanisms can be smoothed and polished. Do **not** have the trigger weight lightened, **only** the action polished.

In addition to trigger smoothing (**not** lightening), semi-autos can also have a "reliability package" done to increase the ammunition's feeding reliability, and can have the triggers converted to double action only (Some manufacturers such as SIGArms[10] have models that can be converted to double action only by swapping out a few parts). The conversion to double action only is acceptable, because it adds an additional level of safety and increasing safety is not a negligent act.

For safety, reliability, and liability reasons, it is important that all modifications and repairs be done by the original manufacturer or a qualified gunsmith.

Double Strike Triggers

Some double action guns have a trigger design that allow double strikes, where in the event of a misfire, a second pull of the trigger will strike the bullet again. Although some U.S. military units still require this feature in issued handguns, I don't see a lot of value in this capability for the average citizen. If you are using a quality gun that is in good condition and are using quality ammunition, the gun should go bang. If it doesn't, there is either a problem with the ammunition or the firing pin/striker. If it happens once, it is most likely the ammunition. If it happens more than once with quality ammunition, it is most likely the gun.

If you are in a gunfight and the gun does not fire, the best thing is to perfor the 'tap and rack' — **tap** the magazine in with the butt of your hand and **rack** the slide, which will eject the current round and load another round. If you have a bad round, a second strike will probably not help, just as with a bad gun. If the gun was not loaded or not loaded properly, or the magazine was not seated properly, the only solution is to 'tap and rack'. Chances are, if your gun does not go bang, you won't immediately know what the problem is, and therefore the reasonable action would be to tap and rack, as it is the best solution for both a bad round or an unseated magazine. Double strike capability is not even useful on the practice range, because ammunition failure is a great way to practice the tap and rack technique.

Safeties

The issue of whether to use a gun with a safety or without is a sticky one as both arguments have merit. Semi-automatic firearms

Safety on a Smith and Wesson auto.

with single action triggers (and some double action) have manual safeties which need to be disengaged before the gun can be fired. Safeties are used on this type of gun because the single action trigger can be easily fired with just relatively light pull with minimal travel. Guns with double action triggers *usually* do not have an additional, manual safety (although some do) because the long, heavy pull of the double action trigger itself acts as a safety, requiring a deliberate pull to fire the gun.

One disadvantage of using a gun with a manual safety is that it is one more thing to remember to do. The fear is that you may forget to disengage the safety when you need the gun the most. This can be overcome with extensive training, but it takes lots of training to make it a natural movement, and the skill needs to be maintained constantly. Many people prefer a double action gun with does not require anything other than a pull of the trigger, so they don't have to worry about forgetting it in a defense situation.

The advantage of a gun with a safety is that it will be harder for a bad guy to use it against you if it is taken away from you. Many police officers have been killed by their own gun. Studies have shown that it takes 2-3 seconds for a bad guy to fire a gun taken from an officer if it does not have a safety. That time increases to 17 seconds to fire a gun taken from a victim after trying to figure out how to disengage the safety. In a gunfight, 17 seconds is an eternity. It gives you time to run, hide, fight, use a second weapon, or disarm the attacker.

A safety is vital for a police officer whose gun is exposed and visible. For the rest of us, a manual safety is another element to add to the list of personal considerations.

If you have a gun with a safety, **do not defeat it in any way!** I have seen some people deactivate the grip safety on 1911 type pistols because they felt that it increased reliability. The backstrap grip safety is perfectly reliable if the gun is in good condition and you use a proper grip. If you cannot get a consistent, proper grip you need to change your carry position, holster or gun. If your gun has a safety, use it! With a defeated/unused safety, a hostile prosecutor could paint you as a negligent gun owner, due to unsafe gun handling techniques. Once it is proven to the jury that you were negligent on one issue, you will probably be considered by the jury to be negligent on **all** issues. Say "Hi" to your cell mate Bubba for me.

Trigger shoes

Shoes are pieces of metal that attach to the trigger to widen it. With the pounding of the gun firing, they tend to loosen and can easily jam the gun.

Aftermarket parts

If any integral part needs to be added or replaced, use factory parts. Don't let the prosecutor tell the jury that you think you know how to make a gun better than the manufacturer. In the eyes of the jury, it can make you look pompous, arrogant, and negligent. Additionally, most factory parts are usually better made than aftermarket ones.

Accessories

The 'no aftermarket parts' rule is for integral parts which affect the functioning of the firearm. The exception to this rule is accessories such as sights, grips, triggers, and lights. There are a wide variety of accessories manufactured by aftermarket companies that offer options not available from original manufacturers. Sights and grips are often as good or better quality that the originals, and the aftermarket certainly has a much wider variety of styles than what are offered on stock guns.

I add triggers to the accessory list, because there is a wide variety of trigger lengths available for 1911 style guns which may be a better fit than stock. My 1911s have all had the stock triggers replaced with short triggers. For large hands, long triggers are available. As with all repairs and modifications, only a qualified gunsmith or the original manufacturer should replace triggers.

Sights

There are two main types of sights: fixed and adjustable. Within those two categories, there are post & blade, 3-dot and partial bar (some other variations may also exist). There are also night sights options.

Outline of the user's view of a standard post and rail sight and a 3-dot sight.

Adjustable sights allow critical sight adjustments. These are used by all serious target shooters. Most adjustable sights are fine for casual shooting but should not be used for carry guns, as they are

Bar sight by XS Sight Systems.

typically more fragile the fixed sights. The last thing you want in a gunfight is to have broken or missing sights. The exception is adjustable sights that are designed for carry. Novak[11] and a few other companies offer adjustable combat sights that work great.

Fixed sights have a much lower chance of breaking than most adjustable sights because there are no moving parts. Instead, they require some changes on the part of the shooter when the target distance changes. Since the sight sits above the barrel, there is a small amount of parallax that makes the gun aim perfectly at only one distance. Picture an "X" laid on its side. The intersection represents the point of aim at the "perfect target distance". From the 'X' you see the shot placement travel higher along the axis as the target is closer, and lower as the target is farther away. This translates to the gun needs to be aimed slightly lower for closer distances, and slightly higher for longer distances. For self-defense, these changes are relatively minor and will have no effect on average defense distances, which are so close.

As for the type of sight, post & blade is the most accurate, since less interpretation is needed by the eye to read the sight. Painting the front blade white or a florescent color can make it easier to see in all lighting conditions.

3-dot sights are pretty much as accurate, certainly more than what is needed for personal combat. I prefer these because they offer faster acquisition for both carry use and action shooting competitions.

Bar sights replace the rear sight with either a vertical bar or two horizontal bars in which the front sight (usually a dot) is centered. While fast, I find these are not as accurate at longer distances because of the difficulty in determining exactly where the front sight should align with the rear. If you don't plan on practicing or doing target shooting beyond 20 feet, these may make very good defense sights for you. More than one shooter, however, has advised me that they have no problems with bar sights and find them very accurate. Must be that 'personal preference' thing again!

Night sights are available in all of the above configurations and are highly recommended. Mostly used in 3-dot style, they incorporate a small amount of radioactive tritium, which glows in the dark. They typically last for 10-12 years before dimming to the point where they need to be replaced. Night sights are relatively dim and the glow is only visible in very low levels of light. The better models have the tritium inserts slightly recessed, so that even the dim glow is visible to the shooter and does not spill out to the sides. In daylight, night sights appear as standard dot sights. I highly

Night sights by Trijicon.

recommend them because a majority of gunfights occur in low-light situations. Whether you ever have a gunfight in the dark or not, having them can't hurt. Typically about $100-$125, many gun manufactures offer models with night sights as an option. If not, a competent smith can add them to almost any gun. TIP: If there is a choice, have the front dot a different color than the rear, because in complete darkness, it is quite possible to hold the front sight to either side of the rear, making it appear that all 3 dots are lined up properly when, in fact, the front dot is not between the rear dots.

Fiber optic sights are relatively new. The fiber optic sight usually replaces the front sight and utilizes the existing rear sight — some replace both front and rear. The fiber optic front sight typically consists of a frame which holds a piece of fiber optic tube. The fiber optic tube collects light and directs it toward the front end of the tube offering a very bright, fast and easy to see dot. Working best in bright sun, it will, however, also work better than a standard

Truglo fiber optic front sight.

sight during dusk and dawn. While fantastic for competition, do **not** use if on a defense gun as the fiber optic tube is fragile. I have had to replace the tubes after about 800 rounds in my competition guns because of breakage problems caused by recoil. **NOTE**: Recently 'combat' fiber optic sights designed for carry have come to market. Time will tell if their increased strength will hold up.

Grips

Like people, grips come in lots of sizes and shapes. Wood, plastic, and rubber are available for just about every gun. I prefer rubber because I get a better grip, particularly with sweaty hands, although they also stick more to covering garments, which can reduce concealability. Depending on what is supplied with the gun,

you may be able get both smaller and larger size grips. Some grips are available with finger grooves to give you a slightly tighter grip since the fingers fit in between the groove. They are beneficial for target shooters, but I dislike them for defense use. The nature of defensive shooting is speed. When your life is in danger, you will draw your gun and grip it fast. The faster you move, the better your chance of getting a poor grip on the gun. A poor hold on the gun may work OK with standard grips, but may be almost

Just a few of the many available grip options for a Smith and Wesson J-frame revolver.

impossible to deal with on a grip with finger grooves.

To demonstrate what I mean, reproduce a poor grip by placing your fingers on a set of standard gun grips with your fingers about a quarter inch lower than they would be when using a proper grip. Then, dry fire. Do the same with a set of grips with integral finger grooves. The difference will be quite apparent.

TIP: If rubber grips are not an option, such as on a polymer frame, use self-adhesive sand paper on the grip to substantially increase your ability to control the gun, especially with sweaty hands. You can use skateboard tape found at sporting good stores or stair tread tape from hardware stores.

Ported/Compensated Barrels

A ported barrel or an add-on compensator has holes in the top to direct exhaust gas upwards in an effort to reduce recoil. While they do work for that purpose, ported/compensated guns are not a good option for self-defense. The problem with them is that the gas that escapes upwards is burning. Known as muzzle flash, the bright light directed upward will reduce your night vision capability. Statistically, most gunfights happen in reduced light, and this is not a good time to have a bright flame temporarily blind you. Additionally, since many gunfights are

Ported barrel on a revolver.

at very close distances, you might need to fire your gun while held close to your body, in order to keep the gun from being snatched by your assailant. In this case, a ported/compensated barrel will cause extensive burning as the muzzle flash projects upwards.

Laser Sights

Laser sights have recently become quite popular. They offer some unique and valuable benefits, but you have to be careful to train and practice with them, and to use them properly. As we have all seen in the movies, laser sights project a red dot onto the target. Their greatest advantage is that they offer a sighting method where traditional sights may not be accessible. Lasers will allow you to aim your gun even if you are not able to line it up with your eyes, such as over and around objects and behind your back. While it might sound absurd to shoot that way, there is more than one story of a victim having successfully used a laser sighted gun to shoot a criminal while the shooter's hands were tied behind his back or otherwise used in a non-traditional shooting position. Additionally, lasers offer a tremendous deterrent factor. An assailant may very well be less inclined to continue his actions when seeing a laser dot on his chest.

One problem with lasers is that they can induce a tendency in the user to ignore the gun's sights. There are several reasons that relying on a laser as a primary sight can be a bad idea. 1. The laser may be broken or have a dead battery forcing the shooter to waste valuable time searching for an aiming dot that is not there. 2. The laser may be blocked either by the shooter, or by an object between the gun and the target. 3. The laser works best in reduced light conditions and may not be visible during the day depending on the brightness of the laser and the amount of daylight. 4. Red clothing may make the laser invisible, since the color of most lasers is red.

The solution for these problems is to use and train with the laser as a confirming sight rather than a primary sight. Continue to use your gun's sights and **confirm** your aim *through the sights* with the laser. The other solution is to train both ways, some with just the laser, some with your gun's standard sights.

Laser designs are available both as integral or attachable designs. Many firearms are being manufactured with accessory rails which offer a great way to attach a flashlight or laser. Keep away from the lasers that bolt on to the trigger guard, as there is not enough support to keep the laser from becoming misaligned. Integral laser designs include grip mounted and guide rod designs. LaserMax[12] offers a replacement guide rod with a built-in laser. Seemingly a great design upon first glance, there have been reported cases of the guide rod breaking and locking up the gun.

Crimson Trace[13] offers lasers built into replaceable grip panels. Available for both autos and revolvers, the grips are offered in hard plastic and some models are also offered in my preferred choice, rubber. The location of the laser makes it prone to being blocked by the trigger finger when it is pressed against the slide or cylinder. You must train yourself to either cup your finger to let the laser pass through or place your finger in a location that does not block the light. This seemingly unfortunate placement can actually be an advantage.

Crimson Trace laser grip on a Beretta.

The Crimson Trace laser is activated by a pressure switch on the grip beneath the trigger guard or on the side grip panel depending on the model. The idea is that your finger would press against the switch to turn it on when needed and relax it's grip when the laser is not needed. Reality though is somewhat different — in a life or death struggle, you will be gripping your gun with a tight grip. Manipulation of your fingers to turn the laser on or off will be impossible, especially so with a two-handed grip. The solution, and this is where the location of the laser emitter becomes a benefit, is to use your trigger finger to block the light. Simply place your finger on the frame or cylinder in a position to block the laser if you don't want it and move it downward away from the laser if you want to use it. It will be unblocked when you move your finger to the trigger, but since the only time your finger should go to the trigger is when you are going to fire the gun, the laser should not be an issue at that point.

Bend your finger and place it on the cylinder/slide to let the laser pass through.

Use your finger to block the laser by placing it on the cylinder/slide in front of the emitter.

Rail mounted lasers mount to the front of the gun under the barrel on the accessory rail. There may be a couple of disadvantages to this design; They do add some weight to the gun and if you intend on carrying it on your gun, you need to find a holster that is designed to fit the gun and laser combination. Rail mounted lasers usually have an on/off switch on their rear. I prefer a design that offers both an intermittent and a constant setting. Be sure your trigger finger is long enough to easily reach the switch.

Regardless of which design you choose, be sure that there is an easy way to control the laser. If the laser is constantly on with no way to control it, the light may give your position away.

Front and rear view of the M6 rail mounted light and laser combo by Insight Technologies.

Sixteen   # CONCEALED CARRY

The good news is that there are many ways to carry a gun. The bad news is that all of them have drawbacks, and none of them work for every person on every occasion. While it is best to carry the same way every time, many people carry in different locations in different holsters, based on their needs and the circumstances of the moment.

The belt is the most popular method of carry because it is very comfortable, and there are lots of holsters available for this

location. Most people wear belt holsters on the dominant side, just behind the hip. The draw is a little faster if worn directly on the hip, but I find it uncomfortable, and it doesn't conceal quite as well there. I position my holster as far back as I can without feeling the butt of the gun pushing into my back when I sit. It winds up sitting at about 4 o'clock. The advantage of this position is it's comfort, but there is one drawback — drawing from a seated position requires that the body be leaned forward in

Fist holster worn slighly behind the hip.

order to reach the gun. This can be quite awkward, especially in a car with a seatbelt on.

Inside the waistband, or "IWB" holsters are the most concealable style, because they pull the gun in tighter than other designs and most of the gun is hidden inside the pants, leaving nothing showing beneath the belt. With an outside the waistband belt holster, you need to conceal both the butt of the gun, as well as the portion of the holster that hangs beneath the belt. I prefer IWB holsters because I like knowing that there is nothing below my belt to be exposed if my vest or jacket rides up too far. With an IWB design, you still need to be careful how you move, but not close to the extent of an outside the waistband design.

To aid reholstering, it is important

Inside the waistband holsters such as this Fist holster offers the best concealment.

that your holster remains open against the pressure of the belt. For an IWB design, the throat needs to be reinforced to keep from collapsing. Otherwise, you will not be able to reholster without holding it open with your other hand, which is difficult and dangerous. Additionally, if the holster goes completely flat against your body, you will probably have to remove the holster in order to reholster the gun.

It is very difficult to reholster if the holster is collapsed by the belt.

A reinforced holster keeps the holster open for easy reholsteing.

To wear an IWB, you need to have the waist of your pants and your belt about two inches bigger than normal. I wear an IWB design for 8-12 hours a day without discomfort. If you get a good quality holster and your pants and belt are the right size, IWB holsters can be comfortable. It is, however, a very personal decision — some people find IWB carry uncomfortable no matter what holster they use and where they position it.

Cross draw holsters sit on the support hand side, in front of the hip. Their biggest advantage is that they offer quick draws from both a standing and seated position, and are a particularly good solution for use in a car.

One disadvantage of the cross draw is that you have to be particularly careful not to point the weapon at your own body or that of bystanders during a draw. The only way to draw from a cross draw holster without lasering yourself is to raise your support

Cross draw holster is worn on the support hand side. (Desantis holster shown)

arm. You need to take extra time to train to do this because it is a somewhat unnatural movement. In relation to bystanders, if you draw straight across from your hip to your target, you will cross all bystanders between your side and your target. To be safe, it is imperative to point the muzzle downwards, not out, as your move the gun to the target. Again, some extra training in this area is important.

I find cross draws a little more difficult than dominant side draws because the rotating momentum of the sideways (cross) draw needs to be stopped before you shoot. It therefore also lessens the ability to point shoot. One last concern is concealability. Cross draw holsters conceal just as well under a shirt as any other belt holster, but if you prefer vests, cross draw is not the best location. This is because your vest will move as your body moves, and these movements or even the wind can easily open the vest far enough for your gun to be exposed. As long as you understand their limitations, cross draw holsters can be good solution.

Shoulder holsters are pretty much the same as a cross draw holster but are located higher on your body. They do, however, look cool on TV. They have the same advantages and disadvantages as the cross draw, but shoulder holsters have two additional drawbacks — the holster hangs where your arm wants to be, which makes it uncomfortable for me, and the hanging design allows the gun to swing side to side and back & forth. Imagine yourself running, with a 2-pound metal block smacking into your arm and side.

Shoulder holsters are great for use in a car. (Desantis holster shown)

Shoulder holsters are good in the car, as they are less likely to get tied up in the seatbelt compared to belt holsters. One area where they shine, believe it or not, is in a public restroom. With any holster on the belt, the gun and holster can be exposed when you drop your pants to the floor.

Center carry places the holster in the center, or slightly off center, of the pants, where the belt buckle usually is, requiring moving the belt buckle off to the side. It really is just a modified version of the cross draw, with the same advantages and disadvantages. You can only carry a small gun there if you plan on sitting down, but I do like it because I find a draw from center carry a very natural movement.

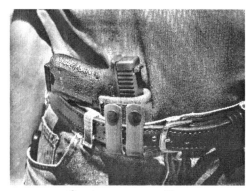

Center carry position.

Small of the back (SOB) holsters place the gun in the middle of the back. As you reach behind yourself, the direction of your hand may need to rotate depending on whether the gun is designed to be holstered butt up or butt down. The center of the back was the preferred place for World War I trench raiders to carry their holstered 1911s, but only because that was the only place where crawling soldiers could keep their weapons somewhat clear of mud.[14] For everyone else, this method holds only disadvantages. It is uncomfortable to sit, hard to conceal, and a far reach is required to move the gun around your body in an unnatural and awkward movement. Most importantly, I feel the SOB carry should be avoided at all costs because if you fall on your back with a gun lodged against your spine, you will most likely end up paralyzed.

One of the best-kept secrets in holster placement is pocket carry. There are two big advantages to pocket carry: 1. You can carry anywhere you wear pants or even shorts and do not want to worry about concealment clothing. I pocket carry to business meetings in a suit, and to the store in shorts. 2. The draw can be very fast. If you anticipate trouble in any sense, you can put your hand in your pocket and grip the gun for a very, very fast draw. Putting your hand in your pocket is very natural and is non-threatening — Nobody will know that you are preparing to defend yourself.

Pocket carry offers great concealment and a fast draw.

While many people simply put a small gun in their pocket, it is essential to use a holster. The benefits of using a holster include keeping the gun from rotating in your pocket, keeping it cleaner (less pocket dust), and reducing the 'print' of the gun. 'Printing' is having the outline of the gun show through the cloth. A gun in a pocket will print like a gun, whereas, a gun in a quality pocket holster should look rectangular, more like a wallet. You can easily carry a small 5-shot revolver in a pocket. I often carry a steel .357 in a pocket holster for 14 hours a day without anyone knowing it and without being uncomfortable. It works great in any kind of pants as long as you have pleats and large pocket openings. You need to make sure the gun sits low enough in the pocket so that the butt will not be visible from the pocket opening. A tailor can easily add extra length to any pocket. Make sure the pocket holster allows an unobstructed grip on the gun (as always) and that it has some kind of mechanism that allows you to draw the gun while leaving the holster in the pocket. This could be a protrusion on the holster that catches on the inside of the pocket as the gun is drawn, an area on the holster that allows your finger to hold it down as you draw, or simply a holster that is somewhat loose and has rough leather on the outside.

The drawbacks to pocket carry are that it is difficult to draw while sitting, and impossible to reach with the support hand.

As many people love ankle holsters as hate them. In reality, they don't work well, even for a back-up gun. The biggest problem

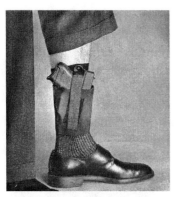

Galco ankle holster.

is that you have to be completely stationary in order to draw from an ankle holster. You can't draw while moving to cover or while running. Even if you are able to be still for a draw, they are slow, because you are required to bend over then raise your pants in order to draw.

Many people think ankle holsters are good for use in a car, but in reality the position is too awkward and slow to be useful. Try this: sit in your car with a dummy or **unloaded** gun in an ankle holster. Pretend that you are being attacked by having a friend run from a car that is parked in front of you, to your car. See how long it takes you to draw your gun from the ankle holster, compared to how long it takes the person to run to your car.

Additionally, ankle holsters take getting used to, as that much weight on the bottom of your leg is very noticeable. They need to be kept tight against your leg in order not to drop or shift while walking. There is a also a possibility of the ankle holster being exposed if your pants ride up when sitting. One trick is to wear a 2nd sock over the holster so all you see is the sock unless you look closely.

Some concealment methods require two hands to draw. These also often require exaggerated motions to ensure clearing of the holster during a

To utilize an ankle holster, you must first completely stop moving and lift your pant leg in order to draw.

draw. If you wear a long sweatshirt to cover a belt holster, you can reach your gun in two ways: 1. Slide your gun hand up your leg to the sweatshirt and pull it up high and then quickly lower your hand to the gun. I find this awkward and would not want to rely

One method to draw from under a shirt is to lift the shirt high with the gun hand, then lower the hand to grasp the gun.

Here, the support hand lifts the garment high above the gun.

on it in an emergency. 2. The support hand reaches around the body, pulling the concealment garment high above the gun. While this "gross movement" is more reliable than the one-handed lift, I don't like techniques that require two hands. In the event that my second hand or arm is busy fending off an attack, carrying a package or child etc., the draw may be considerably slowed by my first needing to free the second hand.

We have spent the better part of our lives training ourselves not to drop things. With all that repetitive training, dropping an object in order to assist the draw is no longer a natural movement — quite the opposite in fact. It may take a deliberate thought process in order to free up the support hand, hence, slowing the draw. I discovered this in the car while trying to swerve away from a driver who pulled out too far into my lane. As I dodged the other vehicle, I never gave a thought to dropping the can of soda that I was holding. This well-entrenched response may very well impede the ability to do a two handed draw if the second hand is occupied.

My preference is to use carry methods and concealment clothing that utilize gross movements of only one hand to reveal the gun, such as a vest or pocket. This way, I don't have to worry about needing to drop anything that may be in my hand. Additionally, my second hand remains free if needed for defense in order for me to get into a position to draw my gun.

To draw one handed from a vest, first swing the vest backwards then bring the hand down to the gun. Be sure to swing the vest back far enough to allow your hand to reach the gun.

When you carry, you always need to be sure you do not inadvertently expose your gun, holster, or spare magazines as you move, walk, and especially as you lift your arms. Belt side holsters require longer cover compared to IWB, because the holsters hang down below the belt.

Most vests found in stores are too short for use as concealment clothing. Sources for good vests and other concealment clothing include specialty companies such as Concealed Clothiers,

While a short vest might appear to keep your weapon covered, simply moving your arm upward can expose your gun.

www.concealedcarry.com, and Coronado Leather, www.corondado leather.com. Photographers vests found at camera stores and 'safari' vests sold at outdoor specialty companies typically are straight on the bottom and make great concealment garments, but can scream "gun" if worn in an inappropriate setting such as a hot day in the summer when everyone else is wearing shorts and t-shirts. You can also buy 'long' size, dressier vests at big & tall shops.

If I am wearing a lightweight vest, to assist the motion of the vest being pushed back during a draw, I add weight to the pockets to help them flap backwards. Ten or so quarters in each pocket helps the drawing of both the gun and replacement magazines.

Seventeen ALTERNATIVE CARRY CONCEPTS

I define anything other than a traditional holster as an 'alternative carry concept'. Often times a normal holster just won't do — whether because of temperature; heavy coats cover the holster during the winter or it's too hot to wear a concealment vest, or environment; concealment vest/jacket would not blend in with the crowd, or any other reason, there are a various other choices for carry.

Vests can be used not only for concealment of a belt holster but to actually carry a firearm as well. Coronado Leather[15], Royal

Robbins, and other manufactures make vests with concealment pockets designed to carry removable Velcro holsters. Coronado vests are fashionable casual wear that do not have a 'tactical' look to them. A person bumping into you innocently would probably not recognize the feel of the gun in a

Vests by 5.11 Tactical (Royal Robbins) and Coronado Leather.

vest pocket as easily as when worn in a belt holster. When carrying a heavy object such as a gun in a pocket, it is best to place either a second gun or extra ammunition in the opposite side to balance the load and keep the vest sitting straight. The only disadvantage of this type of carry is that the vest moves as you walk and therefore the gun is not always in the same place which may slow your draw.

The 5.11 Tactical[16] clothing line offers a casual shirt with two concealment pockets. The opening of the pockets are invisible to the casual observer. A great way to

5.11 Tactical shirt.

carry a lightweight gun, it does print if you look hard enough but it is not easily recognizable as a gun. Not the fastest draw but the 5.11 shirt is great alternative way to carry if a holster is not an option.

Increasingly popular, waist packs (also known as "fanny packs") are a good alternative to a traditional holster. The only disadvantage is that it requires two hands to draw quickly. You *can* open them with just one hand, but it slows things down. These packs come in small, medium, and large, to fit any size handgun. Closure is by zipper or Velcro. I prefer a zipper because

Galco waist pack.

you may not want a loud Velcro noise to alert anyone that you are drawing a weapon. Like other holster designs, there are good ones and there are bad ones. The most distinguishing difference is the how securely they hold the gun. Avoid ones with a generic "pocket" that holds many different gun models. These may not fit your gun tightly, and while the gun may stay in place during normal movement, it may very well fall out during a draw, while running, or even just while leaning over. So far, the best that I have found is the type that uses a wide neoprene belt to secure the gun, such as the ones manufactured by Galco[17]. A very important additional consideration is zipper quality. Compare models and make sure you get one with a smooth zipper. The larger the teeth, the more reliable it will be.

Deep concealment holsters place the gun deep in the pants under the belt or under a closed shirt. The advantage is that they allow carry where no other location may work, however, they are slow on the draw.

Thunderwear deep concealment holster.

One example includes Thunderwear,[18] or similar, which is a pocket worn inside the pants, in front of the crotch, deep under the belt. It takes two hands to draw — one to pull the pants outward, the other to reach in to grab the weapon. I have seen people who can comfortably carry a full-size gun there without it showing. Others, including me, can't carry even the smallest gun there without it "printing" — looking exactly like I am carrying a gun. Make sure that you can return the holster if it doesn't work for you and test it while walking, sitting, and driving, etc.

A similar concept, the PagerPal[19] is a deep concealment holster that slides inside the pants and attaches to the belt by a fake pager. One hand pulls the pager up, the other reaches for the gun. Some say they work great, and others say they don't. They are awkward, at best, from a sitting position. Again, make sure it is returnable.

PagerPal.

A bellyband is a wide strip of elastic with a pocket that you wear under a shirt in the front. The shirt needs to be at least a size larger than normal, needs to be thick enough so it doesn't 'print,'

Galco Belly Band.

and cannot be transparent for obvious reasons. Drawing from a bellyband requires you to first lift or open your shirt.

TIP: If you are using a bellyband with a button down shirt, sew pieces of Velcro where the button should be and then sew the button to the outside of the shirt to make it look normal. The Velcro is an easier, faster, and more reliable way of opening the shirt. Such a small piece of Velcro probably won't be noisy enough to be noticed. Wearing an undershirt beneath the band increases comfort but is a little warmer.

Kramer Handgun Leather[20] makes a deep concealment shirt that places a gun under the armpit. It works OK for a light weight gun, but it is slow. You need a way to lift or open your shirt quickly to access the gun. Use the Velcro here too.

Deep concealment is a good way to carry when no other carry method works — keep in mind though, it is a slow draw, and therefore should be

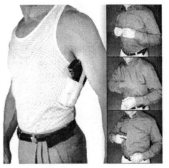

Kramer "Confidant" shirt.

used when you have no other choice or for a back-up.

The last category of alternative carry is off-body. These are holsters that you carry rather than wear. They include bags, briefcases, and the like. One hand holds the case, the second burrows in to reach the gun. As with all two handed draws, it may be difficult or impossible to use if one hand is busy or injured. In my mind, one of the most dangerous parts of using off-body carry is the possibility that the gun inadvertently gets left somewhere. Keep in mind also, if you put it down, it

Defense Planner.

will not be in your direct control. Willfully leaving a loaded gun unattended is a serious safety violation, and could potentially lead to legal and liability problems should it come to the attention of the law.

Eighteen   # HOLSTER DESIGN AND SELECTION

The choice of holster is as important, if not more important, than your choice of firearm. A good gun in a bad holster can be compared to a race car with lousy tires. What may initially seem insignificant is actually a vital part of your safety equipment.

There are many facets to a holster's performance. Obviously, it holds the gun, but it needs to do so properly — not too tightly and not too loosely. If your gun is too loose, at best, it can move and be in a bad position, and at worse it can fall out. I don't want to be put in the position of trying to explain to the little old lady at the checkout counter that I am one of the good guys and that there is no need to worry, as I pick up my gun from the floor. Not to mention trying to figure out what to say to a responding police officer!

A holster that is too tight could prevent a proper grip, throw off your draw, and derail your shooting. I have seen some holsters that were so tight that it was nearly impossible to retrieve the firearm. The better the 'boning', the less tight the holster needs to be. A quality holster is fitted to the gun by boning the features of the gun into the leather, which entails pushing the leather into the feature shapes of the gun with a tool, while the holster is wet and is being formed. A properly boned holster will adhere to the trigger guard, slide stop, safety, and other physical features detailed into the leather. The boning provides the fit around the gun and eliminates the need for a strap to hold the gun in.

Good tests for holster fit are 1. to run at full speed and 2. to jump up and down. The gun should remain firmly in the holster, yet not be so tight as to impede the speed of the draw. If you find yourself tugging too hard to lift your gun, you will need to loosen it. If you have an adjustable holster, the adjustment screw will change the tension easily. If the holster does not have an adjustment screw, and if it is only slightly too tight, there is a simple home remedy. Wrap your gun with plastic wrap, and then several layers of masking tape (I use about four layers) and leave the gun in the holster overnight. The extra thick fit should loosen up the holster. If you don't use plastic wrap first, you may need to get the tape and glue off with some adhesive remover. If one is available, I prefer to use a replica training gun for this purpose. This way, if I don't get all the tape or adhesive off, it's not a concern. If four layers of tape does not work, try again with 8 layers the next night. If that doesn't work, send the holster back to the manufacturer if it's new. If it's too old to send back, you will need to buy another holster.

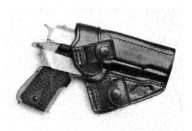

Dummy training gun wrapped in several layers of masking tape to stretch the holster.

In addition to simply holding your gun, the holster needs to do so comfortably. How well the holster and belt supports the weight of the gun has a lot to do with how comfortable your carry rig will be. Thick, supportive leather in the holster — and especially the belt — will keep your gun positioned upright and minimize it flip-flopping around. Nothing is more aggravating to me than my gun flopping around on my belt, not to mention what that does to reduce concealability. For maximum support and comfort, the belt should be thick and sturdy with the holster properly sized for the belt width. If you have a 1.5 inch belt opening in your holster, it won't work well with a 1.25 inch belt. I have seen lots of quality holsters used with wrong sized or low quality belts, only to watch the shooter struggle with draws and reholstering.

The belt loop on holster on the left is larger than the belt allowing the holster to shift position. Correct loop to belt sizing is illustrated on the right.

If all that's not enough, a holster needs to do all of its jobs with a high degree of concealability. This is where things get tricky. Concealability is derived from the person's body size and shape, the holster's placement on the body, and from the size and shape of the gun. What works for one person may not conceal as well on another, and what is comfortable for one, may not be for someone else.

Holsters are variously designed for a 'straight drop,' 'cant forward,' and what some call a 'radical cant'. Some holsters also offer adjustable cants. The forward cant pushes the butt of the gun upward, reducing the amount of the grip that sticks out the back. The greater the cant, the more concealable the gun is, but if its too far forward getting a proper grip becomes difficult. With the more extreme cants, I find it beneficial to bend over slightly at the waist, which offers a better angle to grip the gun. Personally, I find that the best compromise between concealability and access is the 'radical cant,' which angles the gun forward about 20 degrees. It's enough to keep the butt of a full sized gun from sticking out the back, but still allows a good grip.

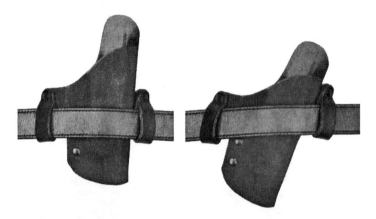

This Fist Kydex holster is highly adjustable. The left photograph shows a straight drop. The photograph on the right shows the holster adjusted with a forward cant.

A more minor design element is the "rise", or how high the gun sits in relationship to the belt. For taller folks, the high rise might be better, but I find I get maximum concealability and minimal movement with standard, non-high-rise designs. The higher that the gun is in relation to the belt, the more flip flop movement there can be. For short people like myself, the added height above the belt makes drawing more difficult, as you have to lift even higher to clear the holster.

One feature that inspires some level of controversy is the thumb break. While they may appear to be essential to hold the gun in the holster, they are, in fact, not necessary for that purpose. Quality holsters retain the gun quite efficiently by their fit and boning. The open top design is a testament to their retention ability. The true intent of a thumb break is to deter a gun grab. The snap reduces the ability for someone to grab your pistol from its holster. While it may be possible for someone else to release the snap, pull the gun through the strap, or even break the holster, the extra safety device does act as a deterrent, slowing down the gun grab or possibly even preventing it totally.

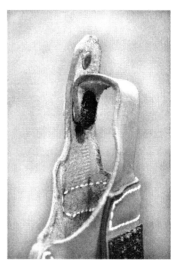

Thumbreak.

The controversy comes in determining if that advantage is worth the trade off. The thumb break does add some time to the draw. With lots of continuing practice, it may add only be a fraction of a second, but it is yet one more thing to practice and therefore one more thing that could go wrong. If you don't practice, you **will** add significant time to your draw at a moment when time is of the essence. Another argument against the thumb break is that if your dominant hand is hurt, using your non-dominant hand (which can be weaker) to draw from a dominant side holster may be made more difficult by a thumb break. This scenario makes a great argument for carrying a back-up weapon accessible to your support hand.

The thumb break question boils down to one question; how likely are you to have someone try to take your pistol from your holster? Compared to private citizens, police officers are far more prone to having the gun taken from them. While the average person may never come into direct contact with a "bad guy" in his/her lifetime, the police officer will. Secondly, the police officer's gun is fully exposed to view, while the average person's gun is usually not known to anyone since it is most often concealed. Most assailants will never know that its there until its too late. An exception to that would be if the altercation starts as a hand-to-hand fight. In the duration of the tussle, the concealed holster is very likely to be discovered even possibly dislodged. In that case, the thumb break may go a long way to delay or completely prevent the gun grab.

Other than that, the average person is not likely to be in a situation where a thumb break would be essential to his/her survival. On the other hand, if you are willing to practice enough on a continuing basis to make the release of the thumb break second nature, it does add one more level of security.

There is no formula for putting all of these elements together. Lots of us have a drawer full of holsters that we like and dislike to some degree. Unfortunately, it's a try and see situation. The good news is that many quality custom holster manufactures accept returns if you are not satisfied. It's worth buying from those companies just for that opportunity, even if you have to pay more.

While leather dominates the market, a new material, Kydex, has made significant inroads in the last few years. Kydex is a plastic material that has good molding and machining qualities. Like almost anything else, there are those who love it and those who hate it. The advantages of Kydex are that it is relatively inexpensive to manufacture, provides a fast draw because there is less friction

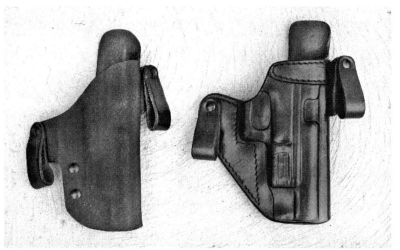

Fist, shown here, and other manufacturers, often offer the same holster design in both kydex and leather.

inside the holster, and it can be designed to be very adjustable.

The expense of Kydex holsters is lower than leather because of the low cost of plastic versus quality leather, as well as the reduction in manufacturing costs and time. Leather manufacturing necessitates that large amounts of the work be done by hand, while Kydex is often machine made. Kydex does not need much maintenance because its plastic. The adjustable tension, found on many Kydex holsters, combined with a design that locks in the pistol but releases as the gun is pulled out allows a fast draw. One of the best features of Kydex is its ability to be designed in a manner that allows tremendous adjustability. Since Kydex is a hard plastic, threaded plates and nuts can be molded in, allowing interchangeable and adjustable belt loops. Some manufacturers offer belt loops of different sizes, so the holster can be used on 1.5 inch through 1 inch belts. Belt loops can be exchanged for J-clips, and it is even possible to change the holster from a belt side to an 'in waist band' design. By placing multiple fastening bolts in different locations, the height of the 'ride' as well as the cant are highly customizable.

There are two disadvantages to Kydex: lack of flexibility and noise. Because the material is a hard plastic, it will never mold to your body with use like leather will. Unlike Kydex, leather holsters tend to become more comfortable over time as they mold to your body. While some people find that Kydex's inflexibility makes the holster uncomfortable, especially when worn 'in the waist band', (IWB) this is not my experience. I often wear an IWB Kydex holster for 8 to 10 hours a day with a full size gun, and find it quite comfortable. Again, personal taste and preference comes into play.

One drawback to Kydex that cannot be discounted is noise. While a leather holster is nearly silent during the draw, the same cannot be said for Kydex. There is slight sound made as the gun rubs against the hard plastic, and there is a definite noise as the gun clears the molded indentations. While this is not too loud, if you need a silent draw, stick with leather.

No matter what material you choose, there are some features that are a **must** for a holster to be considered suitable for carry purposes.

The holster must cover the entire length of the barrel. If not, the front sight can easily catch on the holster as you attempt to draw. You can put a short gun into a long holster, such as a 4-inch gun into a holster designed for a 5-inch,

If the gun barrel extends beyond the holster, the front sight can catch on the edge during the draw.

but not the other way around. There are many holsters out there that have the barrel sticking through. These may be acceptable for range use, but they are not suited for carry use.

A second 'must' feature is the holster's ability to remain open while the gun is not holstered. This is vital because if the holster collapses it will require two hands to reholster. Not only does this endanger yourself because of lasering, it puts you at a severe disadvantage when dealing with an attacker. Holstering a gun into a

This Fist holster features a reinforced opening and body protector.

collapsed holster requires extra attention, and will distract you from your more important task. It is essential that a belt holster be made of sufficiently thick and stiff leather in order to remain open. For IWB use, the holster needs to be reinforced. For the most part, this is not an issue for Kydex holsters, as the stiff plastic remains open. Talk to the holster manufacturer and make sure it fits all of your needs before you buy.

The last, but certainly not least, important feature to look for is the ability to get a full grip while the gun is holstered. A good draw starts with a good grip. Be sure that you can reach around the entire grip and have your hand placed properly up against the bottom of the trigger guard.

One feature that I insist on is a body protector. This is a tang that is extended upwards beyond the side of the holster that rests against the body. Not only does this keep the muzzle from making my shirts dirty, it offers two significant advantages. Reholstering is easier with a body protector because you can motion the gun sideways, pointing downwards, (not towards my body), pressing sideways against the

A properly designed holster does not block the grip in any way such as this Mitch Rosen ARG holster.

protector, and use it to guide the gun into the holster in the proper direction. Secondly, it keeps the shirt from being pushed down into the holster, which would make reholstering or drawing difficult. It also provides an additional advantage for guns that have external safeties, because the body protector prevents your torso from accidentally releasing the safety during normal movement.

Women have additional holster considerations because of their body shape. Often, the placement and cant angle of men's holsters are uncomfortable for women and are difficult to draw from since womens' waist lines are often higher than mens', and may angle inwards. Some holster manufacturers such as Fist, Inc.[21] and Mitch Rosen Extraordinary Gunleather, LLC[22] make holsters designed specifically for women.

I find that with holsters, as with most things, you get what you pay for. The best fitting and most comfortable holsters that I own, I bought from custom manufacturers. They did cost more and I had to wait longer to get them, but I will wear them for years to come. I already have too many holsters relegated to the dresser drawer, not to buy right the first time.

Nineteen   # Competence

Competence is an **absolute must** when it comes to firearms. The more training we do, the more natural shooting becomes. Everyone that owns a gun needs to practice with it often, and be completely familiar with its functioning to the point that it is second nature. When faced with a life-threatening situation, you want to spend all of your efforts on the threat at hand and not on trying to figure out how your gun works.

This goes tenfold for anyone that carries a gun with a manual safety, such as on a 1911 and other similar gun designs. With a manual safety, before the gun can be used, the safety must be moved to the 'fire' position. Every person that I have asked who owns a gun with a manual safety has forgotten more than once to remove the safety before firing during a practice session, myself included. If that happens in real life, it can be deadly. Only extensive practice will make the usage of a gun second nature.

Levels of Competence

There are four main levels of competence that can be applied to all physical movements:

> **Unconscious Incompetence** – means that you do not realize that you don't know how to do something.

> **Conscious Incompetence** – shows a realization that you don't know how to do something.

> **Conscious Competence** – is a state of understating whereas if you think about what you are doing, you can do it correctly.

> **Unconscious Competence** – is an automatic response. You have practiced so often that you automatically perform the required action.

'Unconscious incompetence' is dangerous — reminds me of an old adage: "Incompetent people are too incompetent to know that they are incompetent." When you are at a level of 'conscious incompetence' you demonstrate a respect for the task at hand and a realization that you have to learn about it to become good at it. Reading the safety guide on a new power saw is a good example. You understand that the saw is a dangerous tool and you realize that you need to learn how to operate it safely.

The state of 'conscious competence' reflects the learning process. You know how to do something, you just need to take it slow and think about it to get it right.

'Unconscious competence' is when you have reached the point when muscle memory takes over. You can easily holster without looking. Your finger automaticly disengages the safety when you are ready to fire.

'Unconscious competence' is the level of training **required** to carry a firearm — not just in the firing of the gun, but in all aspects; loading, holstering, drawing, reloading, etc. It takes approximately 3000 repetitions to become unconsciously competent with a specific physical movement. While that may seem a daunting task, if you practice your draw for 15 minutes and do 100 repetitions, it will only take a month to achieve the level of competence required. If you like, stretch out the process; do 100 a day for a week, then 50 a day every other day. Once you have achieved 'unconscious competence' it is fairly easy to maintain your skill level. It has been shown that the more stress you train under, the less repetitions it will take to obtain a high level of competence.

If you ever have to use your gun to defend a life, it is critical to instinctively know how to use it. If you carry a gun with a manual safety, be extra diligent in its use. Practice enough that you learn to keep your finger off the trigger, place the firearm into the ready position, and remove the safety automatically when, and only when, you are ready to fire. Removing the safety too early makes your gun unsafe. Removing the safety too late, or not at all, can make you dead. If you don't or can't practice enough with the safety system to achieve the level of unconscious competence, I strongly recommend using a pistol that does not employ a manual safety.

Manual safety or not, practice until the gun feels like a natural extension of your body — then practice some more.

Twenty DRAW TO WIN

Some say that the first shot wins the gunfight. In actuality, its the first **good hit** that may define the winner. A 2nd and 3rd good hit certainly helps too!

A good hit starts with a good grip. The grip starts at the draw. Following this logic, it is quite possible that your draw could determine the outcome of a gunfight.

Seemingly innocuous on the surface, the drawing of a firearm from a holster is one of the most potentially dangerous elements of gun handling. Speed and safety can be, and often are, diametrically opposed to each other. While speed is necessary (along with accuracy) to get the first shot off to keep the good guy from becoming the victim, speed often leads to improper techniques that put the shooter and/or bystanders at risk. I have heard far too many stories of accidental discharges while drawing a firearm from the holster.

Fortunately, the answer is simple: practice. Sorry if you have heard that mantra too often, but not only does it work, practice is the **only** way of gaining speed while maintaining safety.

I know lots of shooters who, during practice, either shoot from the bench or from a low ready position, but never actually draw from their holster. I can only imagine what will happen if they have to draw their weapon for real. It reminds me of the video of the police officer who took four attempts to draw his weapon when shot at during a traffic stop.

To make your practice session effective, use your carry gun, carry holster, full-power ammunition, and the same concealment clothes that you wear on the street.

As with everything physical, start off practicing new movements slowly — very slowly. Concentrate on performing all of the motions perfectly before increasing speed. The ultimate goal of practicing any physical movement is 'unconscious competence', also known as 'muscle memory', meaning that you have repeated the motion so often that your body automatically knows what to do without thinking about it. The 3000 or so repetitions that it takes to achieve unconscious competence is vital, because you need your concentration to be focused entirely on the threat at hand, not on how to get your gun out of the holster.

Always start practicing new techniques with unloaded firearms. Only when sufficient competence at adequate speed has been achieved, should you move on to live fire. When you transition to live ammunition, start again at very slow speeds. **Always** practice for accuracy. Speed will come with competence. If you are not hitting the 'A' zone with **every** shot, you are going too fast.

For a proper grip, the gun should be placed in the web of the hand in line with your arm's skeletal structure. Your hand should be high on the gun's grip, as the closer your hand is to the slide axis, the more control you have over recoil. Your fingers should grasp the gun tightly, with your middle finger pressing tightly upwards under the trigger guard. If your fingertips are not turning white, you are not gripping tightly enough. Target shooters, not concerned with recoil, prefer a looser grip because it offers better trigger finger control. Defensive shooters are more concerned with recoil control for fast follow-up shots than with finite accuracy, so the tight grip works best.

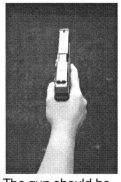

The gun should be placed in the web of the hand in line with your arm's skeletal structure.

Your hand should be high on the gun's grip with your middle finger pressing tightly under the trigger guard.

The support hand should wrap about the dominant hand, high against the trigger guard.

Your support hand should wrap around your dominant hand, high against the trigger guard. The thumb of your support hand should be just in front of your dominant hand's thumb, with the thumb muscle pressing directly against the side of the grip.

Don't just stabilize the gun with your support hand, use it to strengthen your grip. Your support hand should actually tighten your dominant hand's grip by squeezing it. The stronger grip will greatly help recoil control. Some top shooters even go so far as suggesting that the support hand should actually exert more pressure than the dominant hand in a roughly 60/40 relationship. Their reasoning is that reducing the pressure exerted by the shooting hand will give more mobility to the trigger finger, resulting in a cleaner, less jerky trigger press.

In the case of a single action trigger, the trigger should press against the middle of the pad of your trigger finger. For a double action trigger, the longer, heavier trigger is best placed against the first joint. (See photographs on page 63) It is important to get a gun that fits your hand and to use proper trigger placement, because if your trigger placement is not correct, it will throw off your shots.

When learning to draw from a holster, it is best to work in a series of incremental steps to build competence, confidence, and muscle memory. The first step starts from the low ready position. Low ready is used mainly for training and practice, and can also be used when holding a criminal at gun point for a long period of time, because holding a gun up at eye level can be difficult due to its weight. It is amazing how heavy two pounds can feel after holding the gun up for just a few minutes.

Low ready position.

Starting from an upright position, your body should shift its position and weight to a combat position. The support side leg moves forward and apart, and your upper body leans forward to distribute your weight for recoil absorption. The low ready position has the gun gripped properly with both hands, the arms bent at the elbow, elbows in towards the stomach, and the gun pointed slightly downwards so the muzzle is aimed at the ground about 6-8 feet in front of the shooter.

The next step is to extend your arms and raise the gun slowly and smoothly to the target. Ideally, the sights should be lined up with the target by the time the gun is in the final position. The support hand's thumb should be pointing at the target as well. The last movement is to finalize the alignment your sights. Once you are on target and have made the decision to fire, then and only then, should you release your manual safety (if your gun is equipped with one), move your finger inside the trigger guard, and smoothly press the trigger. Practice at least 50, single shots from low-ready before moving on.

The basic extending motion of moving the gun from the low ready to the shooting position will work with the other draw steps. Once you are confident and are getting good shots from the low ready, it is time to work from the chest position. This is where the support hand meets the drawn gun on the way to the final shooting position. Similar to the low ready, the gun is gripped by both hands, but this time you start at the center of the chest. Picture your hands clapping, except that your dominant hand is holding the gun. Just as with the low ready, extend your arms out slowly and smoothly towards the target using your support hand thumb as a guide. Practice at least 50 single shots from the chest position before moving on.

Slow and smooth movement is really the key. The smoother you go, the faster you can hit well. Slow is smooth, and smooth is fast. While that may sound odd, fast movements tend to be jerky and overextend your arms. The resulting shaking and repositioning actually takes more time to correct than if you had drawn smoothly, because a smooth draw means that you won't have to correct and overcompensate for unnecessary movements. As with all physical disciplines, speed and accuracy will come from practice. Once you have practiced enough to be comfortable with the movements and you are hitting the target well, its time to actually draw from the holster and start to put these movements together.

Start with your gun in your holster. Grip the gun completely and properly. If need be, shift the hand to get a proper grip **before** lifting the gun from the holster. Your trigger finger should rest on the slide/cylinder of the gun in the same position it would have if the holster was not there. Grip the gun tightly and get used to the feel. Release your hand and regrip, so you get your hand used to what it a proper grip feels like. This aids in the development of muscle memory.

Holding the gun while in the holster, the first movement is to lift the gun straight up, being sure to keep your finger high on the slide or cylinder. The gun should not angle to either side. It is important not to laser yourself or bystanders, in case of an accidental discharge. As you start to raise the gun from the holster, your support hand should move towards your chest simultaneously, staying tight to your chest to keep it behind the muzzle. Once the muzzle has cleared the holster, bring the gun upwards to the center of your chest to meet your support hand. Once your support hand has gripped your dominant hand, extend your arms forward just as you did in the last exercise.

The last step is to learn to grip the gun from a hands down

position. With your hands at your side, slowly and smoothly follow your leg up to the holster and grip the gun. If you have a thumb break, your hand should travel a little higher than the holster and break the snap as you move your hand down to the gun. Rather than slide my thumb around the grip to break the snap, I find I can get a better grip by moving slightly above the gun then reach down. Practice this movement, feeling for the "proper grip" that you experienced in the previous exercise.

Start from a relaxed position.

Assume a combat position and start to reach for the gun.

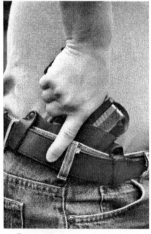

Get a full, proper grip, before lifting upwards.

Meet the support hand at the chest.

Extend towards target while
alaigning sights.

Complete extension and fire.

Put all the movements together, for the final exercise. Remember that smooth is fast and speed with come with practice.

Some shooters prefer a draw technique where the support hand meets the gun near the end of the extension as it advances towards the target rather than close to the chest.

The support hand catches up
to the gun in front of the chest.

Complete the extension and
fire.

The advantage of the first method, where the support hand meets the gun at the chest before advancement, is that it allows for an earlier sight alignment and it works better in confined spaces such as in a car or sitting behind a table. I prefer using a technique that works in the largest number of situations because there will be less chance of a delay caused by the thought and decision making process — No need to ask yourself: "Which draw technique should I use?"

For one-handed shooting, use the exact same procedure, just keep your support hand close to your chest. Clenching your support hand into a fist will induce a sympathetic response in your dominant hand, helping tighten its grip. Some instructors advocate a different foot and shoulder position for one and two-handed shots. Again, I prefer one technique for as many situations as possible, since logic dictates that the less you have to remember to change, the easier it will be to perform under stress.

For one-handed shooting, use the same two-handed position and simply drop the support hand and clench it into a fist at the chest for added strength.

In all likelihood, you will find yourself in a close quarter situation where there may not be room to fully extend your gun or doing so would enable your attacker to disarm you. In that situation, the best draw would place the dran gun slightly in front of your holster tucked tight to your body. The gun should be angled slightly outward away from your body to prevent the slide from hitting your body and potentially jaming it. Your support hand should be used to fend off a direct attack or attempt to give yourself some space by pushing away the assailant. Practice attacking your assailant and defending yourself with your support hand while simultaneously drawing tight to your body with the gun angles slightly to keep the slide from hitting your body.

Fend off the close attack with your hands.

Draw and fire close to your body with the gun angled slightly outward to keep the slide from hitting your body.

These techniques work fine when you have the time to a assume a proper position. In a real-life gun fight, time is a luxury you probably won't have. Once you have built your skills with the proper technique then practice unorthodox methods and positions. One of the best lessons that IDPA and IPSC shooting taught me is that you most likely will need to shoot however and whenever the opportunity presents itself rather than when you and your gun are in proper position!

When you are done shooting and ready to holster, the safety principles still hold. Place your trigger finger high on the slide or cylinder. Move your support hand to a safe position. Rotate the gun downwards at a safe direction and lower the gun straight into the holster at the same angle that you used to draw. Be cautious not to laser your feet, legs and body. Never use your support hand to guide the gun to the holster because it will no doubt get in front of the muzzle putting yourself in a dangerous position in the event of an accidental discharge. If your gun has a cocked external hammer, such as with a 1911, place your thumb on the hammer to keep it from dropping in case of an accident. If your gun does not have an external safety to lock the slide the friction of the holster may move the slide back. To prevent this place your thumb on the rear of the slide to keep if from moving.

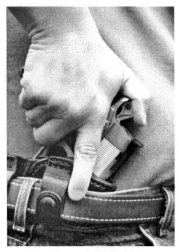

Place your thumb on the
hammer during reholstering
to help prevent an accident.

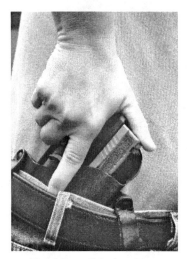

Hold the slide in place
with your thumb during
reholstering if there is no
safety to keep it locked.

Accidental discharges can happen while reholstering because fingers are sometimes left in the trigger guard. Ever hear the phrase; "It just went off"? In reality, the gun fired when the trigger finger was pushed against the trigger as the gun was lowered into the holster.

Train yourself to find a certain finger position on your gun by feel, so you know that your finger is far away from the trigger. On an auto, a good place is the edge of the ejection port; on a revolver, it could be one of the upper cylinder wells.

We all can't get to the range as often as we would like, but you can practice every day. Spend 10 minutes a day doing holster draws and dry firing, and watch your shooting skills soar. Start slow. Keep shooting in the 'A' zone. Speed will come with practice.

Twenty One RELOADING THE FIREARM

Reloading is critical if your gun runs out of ammunition or jams during a gunfight. It is vital to practice reloading and have your technique down pat, because reloading under extreme stress can be very difficult due to of a lack of fine motor control in your fingers caused by BAR. (See Chapter 5 on Body Alarm Reaction for more information).

For a semi-auto, spare magazines should be worn on the support side. My theory is that you cannot have too much ammunition, so I carry two spare magazines. In addition to carrying additional ammunition, it is essential to have a spare magazine to fix a jammed gun. Most feeding problems are magazine related. If you need to remove the magazine to clear the gun, it is often best to use a new magazine rather than the magazine that may have caused the problem in the first place. Additionally, most often the magazine is dropped to the ground when the gun is cleared, and using a fresh, clean magazine is preferable.

The magazine carrier should cover no more than half of the magazine in order to allow a proper grip. The front edge of the magazine(s) should be in the carrier facing toward your belt buckle. If you have a double magazine carrier incorrectly designed to hold one magazine in one direction and another in the other direction, put them both in facing forward. If your double carrier is designed so you are unable to face them both forward, buy another carrier. It is essential that both magazines face the same way to eliminate the fumbling that would result if you had to try to figure out which magazine is facing in which direction. Placing the magazine in your gun backwards may create a serious jam, making your gun completely inoperable during your deadly force encounter.

As an added note: to reduce confusion, never store an unloaded magazine in your magazine holders. This way, you know at all times that the spare magazine you are carrying is loaded.

Before disengaging the magazine in the gun, the support hand should grip the spare magazine, to ensure that there is, in fact an additional magazine available. The support hand should come down over the top of the magazine with the index finger placed along the front edge. Lift straight up to clear the carrier,

The index finger should be placed along the front
edge of the magazine during reloading.

then release the magazine in the gun, letting it fall to the ground.
(While practicing reloads, use a rug or something soft to help break
their fall of the magazine, and clean them often.) The reason that
the index finger is placed
along the front edge of
the magazine is because
your index finger will
naturally travel to your
other hand making it a
great way to guide it to the
gun. As a demonstration:
hold your dominant hand
out in front of your body,
palm   open   vertically.
Hold your support hand
out to the side of your
body, pointing your index

The index finger of the support hand will
naturally travel to the palm of the gun
hand which aids reloading.

finger. Close your eyes and you will see that your pointed finger
will naturally travel to the center of your other hand.

Once the spare magazine is at the gun, place the back edge
of the magazine against the back edge of the magazine well, as a
guide, and slide the magazine in. As the magazine is inserted, open
your fingers and use the palm of your hand to press the bottom
of the magazine flush against the grip. The palm should push the
magazine in with enough force to ensure proper seating. Don't just

push gently until you hear it engage, push it quickly and hard, until it won't go in any further. If you're not sure that it is in completely, hit your palm against the bottom of magazine again to seat it. This is essential because if it is not seated properly, the magazine could drop out.

Guide the magazine into the magazine well. Half way in, open your hand and use the butt of your hand to "slam it home" in one, fluid motion.

Many smaller guns can use the same magazine as their big brother models, with the base of the longer magazine extending below the grip. While this may be fine for practice, the problem is that the magazine could be pushed in too far, jamming the gun. An exception is that some high-end aftermarket manufacturers make extended magazines which utilize a 'magazine stop' to keep them from being over inserted.

Reloading the Revolver

The technique for reloading a revolver varies slightly depending on the type of spare ammunition carrier that you are using. Opposite of a semi-auto, ammunition for a revolver should be carried on the gun side, because revolvers are generally reloaded with the dominant hand. Additional ammunition can be carried in a dump pouch, speed strip, speed loader, or moon clips. Moon clips hold ammunition in a circular ("full moon"), or semi-circular ("half moon") clip and can only be used with guns designed for them. In the case of speed loaders and moon clips, make sure you buy the model designed for your gun, as they are not universal.

Regardless of how you are carrying your spare ammunition, first open the cylinder, shift the gun to the support hand, muzzle pointed up, and with the palm of your strong hand, push down hard on the ejector rod, to clear the spent cases. When empty, rotate the gun and point the muzzle downwards.

In the case of the speed loader, lift the speed loader straight up from the carrier with your strong hand. Line up the bullets with the cylinder and, depending on the type of speed loader, press down to trip the spring or twist the handle to release the bullets. Once loaded, drop the speed loader to the ground, check that the bullets are seated properly, close the cylinder, and switch the gun back to the strong hand. For carry, I prefer the speed loaders that require a twist of the handle to release the rounds rather than the spring-loaded design because the manual twist lock requires a deliberate movement to release the bullets making it less likely to release prematurely.

Speed loaders make reloading revolvers fast and easy.

The same procedure applies for moon clips, but they just drop in and don't require a release mechanism. Speed loaders and moon clips are the fastest and easiest method to reload, but they are bulky, requiring concealment issues to be addressed.

If your gun is designed for them, moon clips are a very fast way to reload.

Speed strips, as the name implies, are strip of rubber which hold the bullets by the edge of the rim. Bullets are loaded into the gun two at a time. Once the cylinder is open and the gun is emptied, retrieve the speed strip with your strong hand, load, drop the speed strip to the ground, close the cylinder, and switch the gun to the strong hand. While not as fast as speed loaders, speed strips are easier to carry and to conceal because of their smaller size. While they do take concentration to use, they are better than not having spare ammunition — but not much better because of how difficult loading becomes under high stress.

While not as fast as speed loaders or moon clips, speed strips are faster and easier than loading revolvers one round at a time.

Besides just loose carry in a pocket, the last option is a dump pouch. The dump pouch, when opened, just 'dumps' the loose rounds into the user's hand to be loaded one by one. Under extreme stress, the difficulty of juggling five or six loose rounds while trying to reload becomes evident.

With both autos and revolvers, once the reload is done, regrip the gun properly, and extend your arms smoothly towards the target to continue shooting or 'cover' the target as you threat scan.

TIP: Dummy ammunition is great for practice off range. You can purchase commercial dummies or make your own if you or a friend have a reloading press. Remove the spent primer from a used case and reload the bullet into the case without powder or a primer. Be sure to paint the bullet head and the bottom of the case to make it easy to identify as a dummy round.

Not only should you practice with dummy loads at home, every time your gun goes empty on the range, you should reload fresh ammunition at full-speed in order to build muscle memory, competence and confidence.

 # AMMUNITION OPTIONS

The choice of ammunition is certainly as important as picking the proper firearm, and can be even more confusing because of the myriad of options. Some people go so far as to state that you should pick your ammunition before your gun, because the ammunition is the most important element due to the fact that it is the bullet that does the work, not the gun.

Once you have a gun, the first consideration is picking the correct caliber of ammunition for your gun. Simply put, the caliber is the size of the cartridge, usually expressed as a number related to its diameter. Examples include 9mm (shorthand for 9mm Luger and 9mm Parabellum), .38 Special, .357 Magnum, .40 S&W, and .45 ACP. Most often, the caliber is stamped right on the gun. If not, review the owner's manual or contact the manufacturer to find out the correct caliber. Technically, the issue of caliber is confusing and somewhat a misnomer. 'Caliber' is actually the cartridge's "name" designation, which is merely related to diameter, rather than an exact measurement. .380 ACP, 9mm, .38 Special, .38 Super, .357 Magnum are all shot from a barrel of essentially the same diameter, but the bullets and powder charge are different and they are not fully interchangeable. (You can however, shoot .38 specials in guns designed for .357 Magnum but not the other way around.

Comparative examples of .32, .380, 9mm, .40, .45 .38, and .357.

It is imperative to use the proper caliber and power level for your firearm. If you are not 100% sure of what ammunition you need or what you are buying, ask. If you don't, the consequences could be dire. At a range, one shooter was firing a 1911 made by Colt, and attracted attention because he was firing a round with an unusually loud retort and excessive recoil. When questioned, it was determined that he was firing a cartridge the he reloaded to .45 Colt specifications. Since his gun had the manufacturer's name 'Colt' stamped on the gun and it was .45 caliber, he presumed that he had the right reloading specifications, not realizing that he had incorrectly reloaded the round to that of a high-power round designed for revolvers. The correct caliber and reloading specifications for his gun was .45 ACP, rather than the .45 Colt he was using. Fortunately he was stopped before any serious damage was done to him or his gun.

Once the correct caliber is established, bullet design is to be considered. Most bullets fall into these categories:

> **Wadcutters** are flat nosed bullets that are usually low in power and are designed for target shooting. The flat shape creates very clear holes in the paper for easy scoring. Wadcutters don't work well in semi-autos that are not designed for them because the flat face makes a sharp bullet edge that impedes feeding.

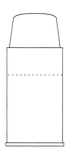

> **Semi-Wadcutters** are a cone shaped version of the wadcutter, typically offering more power and improved feeding in autos. While semi-wadcutters were previously used for self-defense, hollow-points are now the standard.

> **Round Nose**. As the name suggests, the bullet head is round. Also known as ball, or hardball (when jacketed), round nose bullets are fine for practice or target shooting, but have very poor stopping capabilities. The tendency for round nose ammunition is to go right through the intended target with relatively little damage.

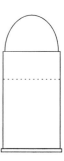

Full Metal Jacket. **(FMJ)** bullets are round nose bullets with a copper-alloy layer covering the lead bullet. The jacket improves feeding in autos, leaves less residue in the barrel, and creates less smoke when fired compared to unjacketed bullets. Like round nose, FMJ bullets are not typically a good choice for defense as the jacket reduces bulet expansion, and may allow the bullet to pass right through the target.

Hollow-Points. **(HP)** As the name implies, the head of the bullet is somewhat hollowed out. Sometimes also known as Lead Hollow-Points (LHP) or Jacketed Hollow-Points (JHP), (depending on type) in most cases, HPs are the best choice for protection. The cavity of of the hollow-point is designed to fill with flesh, which forces the head to expand. The resulting expansion 'mushrooms' the bullet, creating a larger projectile that will do more damage to the assailant's body than a non-expanding round. The more shock that is 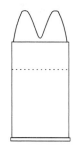 transferred to the body, and the more damage that is done to tissue and vital organs, the better the chance of stopping the aggressor.

WARNING: Be sure hollow-points are legal in your state. New Jersey outlaws them for carry outside of the home, and other jurisdictions may restrict them as well.

Winchester Silvertip shown unfired and expanded.

Jacketed Hollow-Points (JHP) and Semi-Jacketed Hollow-Points (SJHP) are variations of the hollow-point design, that have a metal coating or plating on the bullet head. Depending on the desired performance criteria of the manufacturer, these designs may increase or decrease penetration and expansion.

Expanding Full Metal Jacket (EFMJ) is essentially a hollow-point bullet with a ball inserted in the cavity. When they strike flesh, the ball is pressed inwards which expands the bullet in similar fashion to a hollow-point.

While the EFMJ's round nose profile aids feeding, their main advantage is that they are often legal in jurisdictions that outlaw the use of hollow-points.

Pre-Fragmented / Frangible bullets are designed to break into small pieces upon impact offering good stopping power with reduced penetration. They are a good choice for defense in penetration sensitive locations such as apartments, airplanes, nuclear power plants, chemical plants, etc. Some frangible bullets are made from powdered metal fused together. They impact the target as a solid bullet and disintegrate into dust when they strike a solid object. These are good options for training with steel targets at close distances in order to eliminate richocet.

Full metal jacket round nose, semi-wadcutter and hollow-point bullets. (Images courtesy of Winchester Ammunition)

Power Considerations

There are also power variations to consider as well. A .357 Magnum is basically a .38 Special bullet in a longer case with additional gunpowder. The benefit of this is more power and therefore better stopping capability. The drawbacks are higher recoil, and a greater possibility of over penetration of the target. The .44 Magnum is, likewise, a more powerful version of the .44 Special. You can use .38 Special cartridges in .357s and you can use .44 Specials in .44 Magnum guns, but not the other way around.

Most often seen in .38 Special and 9mm calibers, +P (plus P) designation denotes extra power. The +P+ (plus P plus) designation denotes 'more' extra power. While these loads offer better stopping power, they are very powerful and you should never use +P or +P+ rated rounds unless your gun is designed for them. Always check with the manufacturer to see if your gun can handle the higher power ammunition.

Other Considerations

The choice of ammunition depends on your circumstances and situation. Firearm choice, shooting capabilities, expansion, and penetration requirements need to be factored in.

The number one consideration is your gun's ability to reliably feed the round (in the case of an auto). Since a defense gun must perform flawlessly, test fire an automatic with at least 200 rounds of your carry ammunition. If you encounter any failures to feed, have the gun worked on by a qualified gunsmith, or change ammunition.

Secondly, you need to judge whether or not the cartridge is a good match for the type of gun and your shooting skills. If you carry a lightweight or small frame gun, you may have difficulty controlling your shots if the ammunition is too 'hot' (powerful). If you find it difficult to maintain a proper group on your target, or if it takes too much time to reaim between shots, the ammunition may be too powerful and create too much recoil for you. If this is the case, try a few different types of ammunition and choose a less powerful round that allows you to maintain control.

Generally, within the same caliber, the heavier the bullet, measured in grains (gr.), the more recoil is generated. As a reference, 438 grains equals one ounce. So, a 230 gr. bullet weighs just over one-half ounce. If you find that the recoil generated from a 230 gr. bullet is too difficult to control, try a 180 gr., or even a 165 gr. (Sometimes however, manufacturers develop specialty ammunition that may be hotter or lighter than those of comparable bullet weights, so be sure to test a few different types to determine which is the best fit.) If you are using a +P+ or +P, step down. If you are using .357 Magnum or .44 Magnum, drop down to .38 or .44 Special loads. If the .40 S&W or .45 ACP is too much, try a 9mm. While the smaller or lower power bullets may not 'stop' as well as their big brothers in a 'perfect' situation, the more controllable bullet will offer far better stopping power for you because you will be able to shoot it better. If possible, try borrowing or renting guns of various calibers to see what you can shoot best.

The shorter your handgun's barrel, the less bullet velocity is created, and therefore the bullet will expand less and penetrate less upon impact. Short-barreled guns should be carried with ammunition designed to expand at lower velocities such as non-jacketed, lead hollow-points. The best choice for short-barreled guns for both control and stopping power is lighter, higher velocity ammunition.

If you are in a densely populated location such as an apartment building, frangible ammunition may be your best choice, since the chance of over penetration is greatly reduced. Keep in mind however, that the problem of over penetration won't be completely eliminated, so you still need to be aware of what are you are shooting and what is behind it.

Hollow-points are excellent for use in self-protection because they provide maximum transfer of energy to the body, and destroy more tissue than ball or wadcutter ammunition. While it may seem as though it would be difficult to justify your use of 'menacing — looking' hollow-points to a jury, quite the opposite is true. As a public safety policy, the use of hollow-points is safer because they are less likely to over penetrate and hit bystanders behind the assailant, compared to round nose bullets. With the greater stopping power of hollow-points, fewer bullets will need to be fired, which increases your overall chances of survival. Lastly, every local and federal law enforcement agency uses them. Once again, make sure hollow-points are legal in your state!

Reloads

Reloads are remanufactured cartridges made with used casings. Often made by the hobbyist with a hand-operated reloading press, gun stores often sell commercially produced reloads as well. Reloads are popular because they cost less than new ammunition.

Never use reloads for defense purposes — **Never**. There are a number of reasons for this:

1. Reloaded ammunition is inherently unreliable. Made with used casings, there are often defects in the brass, caused by its continued reuse, which makes them fail. When a bullet is fired, the casing expands due to the internal pressure. Part of the reloading process is to resize them back down to the correct size. This expansion and resizing weakens the metal, which will eventually cause the case to weaken and/or crack, which can result in a blowout which can jam or damage the gun. Additionally, sometimes the resizing is not done properly, which can cause the ammunition to jam the gun. Another common reloading problem is incorrect powder drops, which can cause a 'squib' (too little power), resulting in a bullet lodged in the barrel, or a 'double

charge', possibly resulting in a damaged gun because of too much powder.

2. In the event of a shooting, the performance of reloaded ammunition cannot be tested by police during an investigation, because it cannot be proven as to what components the ammunition was made of. Authorities keep stocks of all manufacturing lots of all commercial ammunition for testing comparisons in shooting investigations. If you use reloaded ammunition, they will not be able to compare your claims against any ammunition test results.

3. In court, the prosecuting attorney may tell the jury that you made your own ammunition because you think you know more about how to make ammunition than commercial manufacturers, and that your goal was to make ammunition that was more deadly than you could purchase. True or not, how do you think that will affect the jury's opinion?

While buying reloads or reloading your own ammunition is less expensive and fine for practice, stick with factory ammunition for self-defense — it is far more reliable, while offering top stopping power.

TIP: After loading your defense firearm, keep the remaining ammunition in the original manufacturer's box and mark it with the date that you bought it, the serial number of the firearm that you loaded it into, and the date that you loaded it so, if needed, you can prove what ammunition you was in your gun. In the legal defense of a shooting, it may be necessary to have the ammunition that you used tested in order to prove your testimony. An example would be if, in your defense, you shot an attacker as he lunged towards you with a weapon from just a few feet away, yet, he testified under oath that you shot him for an unknown reason from across the street. For confirmation of shooting distance, a comparison of powder burns from a immediate distance can be compared to the powder burns (or lack of) of a shot taken from a further distance. This comparison would only be possible if you are able to positively identify and prove what ammunition you used.

Twenty Three

STOPPING POWER

The key concept in the phrase 'stopping power' is just that, to stop; to incapacitate, to prevent your attacker from injuring or killing you. The goal in the defensive use of lethal force is *not* to kill, but to stop an attack. Granted, death may occur as a result of the actions taken to stop the attack, but even the actual lethal wounding of the assailant may not immediately terminate the attack. Just like a chicken running without a head, an attacker with a fatal wound can still retain enough oxygenated blood to have up to fourteen seconds in which to continue the attack. You can still be killed or seriously injured by someone that you have just mortally wounded. *This is worth repeating;* You can still be killed or seriously injured by someone that you have just mortally wounded.

A bullet may have killing power but lack stopping power. This can be best illustrated by a round nose bullet that goes through the body with minimal damage to critical organs or the skeletal structure. The impact and damage done to the body may not be enough to stop the aggression, but the person may bleed to death, minutes, or even hours later.

The study of stopping power is, without question, the most controversial subject in the use of firearms. The controversy is caused by the lack of ability to create scientifically accurate tests. The only truly scientific way to test the effects of bullets on the human body would be to test bullets on a human body. This, obviously, is not an option. Even if it were an option, variable factors such as shot placement, path of bullet, body mass, adrenaline, illicit drugs, and emotional state, etc., cannot be easily computed, much less duplicated.

An attacker will stop for one of three reasons:

1. The damage done by the impact of the bullet has stopped the ability of the brain to communicate with the body, or the skeletal structure has been damaged.

2. Enough blood has been drained from the body to stop its ability to move.

    3. The attacker's reaction to having been shot is to voluntarily stop the attack.

There are a tremendous number of factors that, when combined, make stopping power all but impossible to quantify. People have died from seemingly minor flesh wounds made by .22 caliber bullets, and there are many accounts of attackers continuing their rampage even after being hit with multiple rounds of .45, .357 Magnum and even by shotguns.

Handguns actually have very little stopping power relative to rifles and shotguns. That is because the size of the projectile is miniscule compared to the size of the human body and the shock created by the bullet is restricted by the small size of the cartridge. Shotguns and rifles have far greater stopping power, not necessarily because of their bullet size (some rifle bullets such as the .223 are far smaller than many handgun rounds), but because of the higher amount of momentum and energy transferred by the projectiles due to their high speed. The additional advantage shotguns offer is they fire multiples projectiles simultaneously.

Since we can't count on the sheer power of a handgun bullet to stop a threat by itself, we rely on two factors to increase stopping power: shot placement and firing multiple shots.

To "shut your attacker down" you need to hit the brain or spinal cord. It is not important just to hit something, it is important to hit something important! The damage done by the bullet is directly related to where it impacts the body, and its subsequent path of travel. A hit in the so-called 'critical zones' will produce the most critical bodily damage. Shots to the cranial cavity (between the base of the nose and the eyes to disrupt brain signals) and to the vital organs in the torso, are your best bets to stop criminally violent behavior. While headshots are difficult, if the aggressor is wearing body armor, (disturbingly, becoming more and more prevalent), the headshot may be the only way to stop the attack.

    Hitting small targets like the critical zones is exteremly difficult especially when in a high stress situation. If the bullets do not hit a vital organ or disrupt the brain signals, you will need to rely on blood loss to stop the body from functioning.

    All things being equal, the more holes in your assailant, the better. Multiple wounds increase blood loss and shock to the body. The best placement of multiple shots is not close to each other, as you might expect, because you will just be damaging flesh that has

One or more hits in the critical zones is necessary
to "shut your attacker down".

already been damaged. The best results are achieved with shots placed 3 to 4 inches apart. Don't just shoot and stand there staring, expecting your assailant to fall down; keep shooting until the threat stops. As long at your attacker is capable of moving and still has his weapon, he is a threat. Be aware of the concept of 'excessive force'. If you keep shooting **after** the threat has stopped, you run the risk of being charged with the use of "excessive force" because of the perception that you were trying to kill the attacker, not just stop him.

The psychological effect of being shot can also be a major factor in stopping an attack. After being shot, some people, logically reasoning that the injury sustained and/or the chance of further injury is not worth the benefit of the crime, simply stop their aggression. Keep in mind though, some people will get even madder at being shot, and may continue the fight with increased vigor.

There are even accounts of people, realizing they have been shot, simply falling down and dying, because that is what they expected to happen even though they sustained relatively minor wounds. For this reason, it is essential that you, the good guy, maintain the fight instinct and the will to live. Regardless of the situation, regardless of any injury, keep fighting until your attacker is stopped. Often times, willpower and the instinct to prevail are the most important determining factors of the outcome.

Body chemistry and the presence of illegal drugs can, and do, have a dramatic effect on the body's tolerance of pain and its ability to sustain wounds with seemingly little result. There are many reports of criminals who, having sustained multiple, severe gunshot wounds at the hands of police, kept on fighting. Subsequent toxicity tests reported high levels of illegal stimulants (such as PCP), which kept the assailant from succumbing to, or even noticing the pain.

Ballistic Testing

Body tissue damage and shock to the body is created by transfer of the bullet's energy to the body. This bullet energy is created by a combination of two factors; weight and speed. There are two schools of thought here as it relates to handgun ballistics: light and fast, or heavy and slow. The 9mm is a relatively light bullet that moves at a relatively high speed. Proponents of such calibers claim that the increased speed of light bullets helps with expansion. The slower moving, big bullet proponents assert that big bullets do not need to rely solely on expansion, because the bullet is already relatively large. Both theories can be correct, as evidenced by the .357 Magnum and .45 ACP, both of which have historically proven to be excellent stoppers.

When a bullet penetrates flesh, two types of wounds are created:

1. The "wound channel" itself, in which the flesh and organs are destroyed directly by the bullet.

2. The "temporary wound channel' which consists of the flesh and organs that are affected by the hydrostatic shock waves created by the bullet traveling through the body.

The temporary wound channel helps to account for the high stopping power of rifles. The shock damage done to the body by handgun bullets is a highly debated topic. One theory is that these shock waves have power equal to that of the actual bullet to disrupt and destroy the body, and some even go so far as to suggest that the temporary wound channel can actually do *more* to destroy organs and shut down the body than the direct damage to flesh by the bullet. The opposing theory is that the handgun bullet does not have sufficient power and does not transfer enough energy to create shock waves strong enough to damage the body. This is more evidence that the topic of stopping power is highly controversial.

There are many competing theories of how to measure stopping power. These include ballistics gelatin studies, studying the effects of actual shootings, and animal comparison studies. All of these theories have their strong points, and all have their drawbacks. There is no true standardized scientific manner in which to complete a study of stopping power because of the vast range of variables.

Ballistic gelatin is a medium designed to replicate the soft tissue of the body. Similar to, but much thicker than the kind of gelatin that we consume for dessert, ballistic gelatin is formed in 6"x6"x16" blocks which are fired into for testing of ammunition. A comparison of the resulting bullet expansion, penetration depths, and wound channels are used to compare bullet performance and predict the effects of bullets fired into the body.

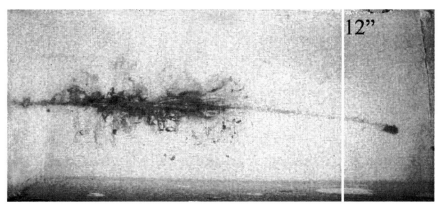

Bullet path, wound channel, and bullet visible in ballistic gelatin. (Photo courtesy of btammolabs.com)

The advantage that ballistic gelatin has that is not shared by any other testing method is that gelatin is homogeneous and consistent, making the test results repeatable. The problem in using ballistic gelatin for testing, however, is that the human body is *not* a homogeneous substance, and different body parts will therefore react differently to being shot. While the performance of different bullets can be compared to each other, the varying quantities and densities of flesh, muscles, organs, bones, and fluids of the body make a fair comparison to gelatin impossible. Additionally, an assailant's mental state, drug use and the like cannot be accounted for via gelatin.

While studying the after effects of actual shootings may appear to be a reasonable method to study stopping power, the shot placement, mental state, body chemistry, and body mass factors still cannot be calculated. Tests on animals can be faulted for similar reasons. The body of a pig does not react in the exact same manner as the human body does, and even if it did, non-repeatable factors such at bullet path, mental state, adrenaline, etc. are not able to be factored in, not to mention that the psychology of pigs is different than for humans, and there's no reason to assume that they would react the same way to being shot.

As much as I would love to tell you which bullets perform the best, the experts can't even agree on what constitutes good performance never mind agree on how to test and compare them. Even if it were possible to realistically compare performance, no bullet is perfect for every situation. What may work well in an up-close encounter may not work if you have to shoot an attacker that is hiding behind a barricade. The same bullet that has sufficient power to get through that cover, may go right through an adversary in the clear and hit a bystander behind.

While much is unknown and unquantifiable in the study of stopping power, and there are many things that we will never know, the good news is that there is one thing everyone agrees on; shoot multiple shots.

While it is best to hit the 'critical zones', it is extremely difficult to hit a small, moving target when you are also moving and experiencing the debilitating effects caused by Body Alarm Reaction. Obviously, you should not ignore shot placement, but don't expect the same marksmanship as on the practice range. The way to compensate for less than perfect aim is to put as many holes in your attacker as possible during the attack. The more holes and the more damage, the higher the possiblity of stopping the aggression. The final word on stopping power is "keep shooting until the threat stops."

Ammunition Choice

Not too many years ago there was a major difference between bullet designs — some performed better than others. Today, that gap has narrowed considerably and quality hollow-point and frangible ammunition are made by numerous companies.

As for bullet choice, any one of the modern, high-performance rounds from today's major manufacturers will be perform adequately. As of this writing, some examples include:

Manufacturer	Models
Corbon	All models including Glaser Safety Slug
Federal	Hydra-Shok Personal Defense
Federal	Expanding Full Metal Jacket
Remington	Golden Saber
Speer	Gold Dot
Winchester	Silver Tips
Winchester	Ranger SXT

There are several bullets that are designed to meet specific performance characteristics such as high penetration or those that have the ability to penetrate glass (windshields) more easily. I don't cover these specialized rounds because, unlike the police or military, the typical armed citizen does not have the need for a specific performance requirement since there is no expectation of a specific kind of attack. While a police officer may have a need for ammunition for a specific unique type of threat, and can change ammunition accordingly, the average citizen is best armed with standard ammunition that can be used in a wide variety of situations.

The most important element of choosing ammunition for any semi-automatic firearm is feeding. Make sure the round you carry feeds **perfectly**. The next most important point is recoil and controlability. Generally, the larger the bullet, the more recoil, however, because of specialty design characteristics, that does not always hold true. Test different rounds in your carry gun and see which you are best able to control.

Choosing a Caliber
In terms of caliber choice, I personally prefer to carry a full size gun in the biggest caliber that I can shoot accurately and quickly. The number one consideration is finding a gun that fits you best,

that you can properly conceal, and that you can shoot well. Most often, different calibers are available for the same model of gun. I recommend that new shooters start with .38 Special for revolvers and 9mm for automatics to learn and build their skills. Because shot placement is far more important than caliber, you should carry the caliber that you can shoot best. Move to a larger caliber only once sufficient shooting skills and recoil control has been achieved.

While there is no perfect test for shooting skills, I rely on the 'Test of 5s'. The goal of the test is to shoot 5 shots, first one drawn from the holster, into a 5-inch target, from 5 yards, in 5 seconds. This test is a good method to determine how well you shoot a particular gun, as a well as being good caliber comparison test.

Not having much luck shooting a Glock well because of my small hands, I compared the results of the Test of 5s with my Glock and a Springfield Armory XD. Right out of the box, first time in my hands, I shot the XD much better than the Glock on the Test of 5s — which is why the XD is now my primary carry gun. I then tested the XD in both 9mm and .40. While the 9mm grouping was slightly better than the .40, the results were close enough, and I chose the higher-powered .40 caliber. Had there been a major difference in group size, I would have chosen the 9mm.

Use the Test of 5s to judge your progress as you train. Be cautious that you don't go too fast and exceed your ability to shoot well, because that is the recipe for an accident.

Another stopping power issue in regards to caliber and gun choice is firepower — the capacity of the pistol. While I am old-fashioned and prefer large bullets, the higher capacity available with smaller calibers makes a very strong and convincing argument. Seventeen rounds of 9mm versus eight rounds of .45 can be a real argument stopper.

I would like to tell you which gun, caliber and ammunition to use, but it's just not that simple — everyone's body, ability, and situation is different. Pick a gun based on what you can shoot well, and choose the ammunition that is perfectly reliable in your gun and best fits your shooting capability.

Twenty Four

STREET TRAINING KEEP IT REAL

Officer Smith is dispatched on a disturbance call. Upon arrival he attempts to interview a known drug dealer who is present on the scene. The suspect threatens the officer, picks up a weapon, and charges the officer in a threatening manner. Realizing that he is in grave danger, Officer Smith draws his department-issued firearm, fires two shots, and then lowers his gun. The suspect sustains two hits to the chest and continues his drug-driven rampage, killing Officer Smith. When hearing this story, most people's first question is, "Why did he lower his gun while he was still in danger?" The almost unbelievable answer is: "He was trained to."

Officer Smith, like many, many other people, spent hour upon hour training to draw, fire two shots, lower the gun, and then reholster. The most important incentive for proper training is the fact that under extreme stress, we will do what we are trained to do.

In reality, not many of us are likely to be attacked by a piece of cardboard that is standing motionless in front of proper backstop with no bystanders in the way — but that's often how we restrict our training. Therefore, the impetus is upon us to adapt our training to make it as realistic as possible in relation to the types of situations that we may actually encounter. Here are some easy ways to make your training sessions better, and prepare you for what you may face in real life:

On the practice range, every situation is usually designed to be a shoot situation. This can create the dangerous mentality that every critical situation requires a resolution by gunfire. Far more important than gun-handling skills, is the ability to determine when to shoot and when not to shoot. Don't train yourself to shoot every time you draw your firearm. Don't make every training scenario a shoot scenario. Be sure to train with designated no-shoot targets, and to place no-shoot targets in a manner that obscures part of the shoot targets. Train as much as possible in both shoot and no-shoot scenarios.

Verbalize on the training range. Envision a real life situation and interact with the suspects accordingly. Practice cooperative situations also. Give disarming orders, and practice commands to put the criminal in a safe position, call police, and to deal with family and bystanders.

Distance, cover, and concealment are your friends. Practice your verbalization and shooting while getting to a safer place. Get

so used to shooting from cover that it feels unnatural to shoot in the open.

Remember the police cruiser video of the officer that took four attempts to get his sidearm out of his holster when attacked on a routine stop? Practice holster draws — If you use a thumb snap holster for carry, use it at the range, and practice unsnapping it. Practice drawing at realistic speed. Draw while moving, while verbalizing, and while interacting with others.

Cars make great cover because they are plentiful and the engine block is inpenatrable to most gunfire. Make yourself as 'small' as possible when using cover.

A miss on the street may kill an innocent or get you injured. Don't just shoot as fast as you can pull the trigger, shoot as fast as you can hit accurately. Don't worry about speed, it will develop with practice. When you miss, use it as a training tool. Was it a flinch? Sights not lined up? Trigger control? Take the time to understand why you missed and how to correct your mistakes.

Find your limits and understand them. Realize that the stress of a real life situation will make shooting much, much harder than during training sessions. In one of my own training sessions, I took five shots at a 'hostage taker' from 30 feet, as the 'criminal' moved out from behind the 'victim'. It seemed like an easy shot at the time. Result: Four nice holes in the 'assailant's' shoulder, one in the 'victim'. Before attempting

A hostage situation is a very difficult scenario because of the proximity of the victim to the assailant.

this in training, I thought that I could make the shots if I ever needed to in real life. It took a hit on the innocent 'victim' on the range for me to more thoroughly understand my limits.

Envision this scenario: you're in the back of a convenience store. You walk to the cashier and realize that there is a robbery in progress. The criminal is holding a gun on the clerk. You draw your weapon and order him to put down the gun. He turns to shoot you. Do you think that you can react fast enough to shoot him first? The only way to know for sure is to act out the scenario with simulated weapons such as airsoft technology, Simunitions[23], or even paintball guns. Train in real-life scenarios with simulated weapons, and find your limits.

On the street, bad guys rarely stand still while you shoot them. Use moving targets. Practice shooting while you move. Use different height targets. Place multiple targets in different locations and at different angles.

Proper training utilizes multiple targets at different heights and angles. Note the targets on the far edges.

The first time I was at a range where I was allowed to shoot at a wall, I found it disconcerting, and hesitated the first couple times, because I spent years making sure that I did not hit a range wall. The first time you are required to shoot at a human being, this may happen to you a hundred fold. Make your targets as realistic as possible, even if it is something as simple as putting a T-shirt over cardboard. You must also be aware of your state's laws. Just as some states deny their citizens the ability to defend themselves with the most effective ammunition, some states prohibit the use of human silhouettes targets.

Placing articles of clothing on the targets gives a more realist appearance.

In real life, you need to shoot until the threat stops. When you shoot on the range, don't simply double-tap the targets, use as much ammunition as you may realistically need in a real shooting. If you're working with pepper-poppers (steel targets that fall when they receive a solid hit), shoot continuously as they fall, and don't stop until they do.

If you have to shoot on the street, chances are it will not be two shots, slow fire. Practice controlled, rapid, continuous fire.

Most gun fights are at close distances, yet little practice is ever done at distances less than 15 feet. Set up scenarios where you fire at targets 10, 5, and even 3 feet away. Practice both defensive and offensive moves where the criminal is close enough to reach you before you shoot.

Practice should include realistic distances including close-up shooting.

After you are done shooting, don't let your guard down. Stay ready to defend against another attack. Keep an eye on the assailant to make sure you are not attacked again. Scan your surroundings and look for accomplices and other threats. Don't just look for a whole person, look for parts of a body — look for feet, hands, weapons, etc.

Don't simply stand behind cover and concealment. Shoot from barricades as if someone is really shooting back. Don't expose any more of your body than you really have to. Shoot over barricades, through them, under them, and next to them. As much as possible, use realistic objects like telephone poles, mailboxes, and especially cars.

After your weapon is drawn, at some point you will need to reholster and deal with the criminal and possible bystanders. While reholstering may seem simple, I have seen more than one weapon dropped or fired while reholstering. Practice reholstering while using only your gun hand and without looking at the holster, so you don't look away and give the bad guy the advantage.

We are all trained to use the sights on our guns. During a draw, I often think to myself; "front sight, front sight, front sight" to remind myself to aim. In reality though, aimed fire may not be realistic. In the heat of a life threatening situation, you will be concentrating on your assailant and his weapon, and not on your sights. More than likely you will be point shooting and not using aimed fire. Point shooting is especially prevalent in quick encounters where a shot is fired as soon as the gun is drawn. Quick point shooting should be practiced, along with aimed fire. Knowing that you can quick fire accurately by pointing will give you added confidence if you need to do it on the street.

If you shoot IPSC or IDPA type matches, keep in mind that some of the techniques that will help you win the match may get you killed on the street. Load behind cover, not out in the open. If you are under fire and slide locked (semi-auto's slide automatically locked back when empty), reload as quickly as possible and skip the IDPA 'tactical reload' which, in reality, is too difficult to perform in a high stress situation. Two 'C' shots may be enough for a target to be considered 'engaged' in a match, but a criminal may still be able to attack you with just a few 'C shots'. Don't hit twice and think you're done. Shoot until the threat stops. For that matter, two 'A' shots may not even be enough to stop the bad guy. The human body can have up to 14 seconds of oxygen after clinical death with which to continue its violent rampage. Keep that in mind, and practice covering all targets until you are sure they have stopped for good.

Practice shooting multiple shots at a fast, realistic speed.

Practice these suggestions and as many others that you can think of, because training works — plain and simple. The first time I attempted shoot/no-shoot scenarios, I was almost in shock. I stood there nearly motionless, my mind racing through all the options and ramifications that I could think of. While my mind was thinking, my body was getting shot. In my next attempt, I was verbalizing, using cover, and taking control of the situation. If just a few minutes of training can have that dramatic of an effect, imagine what the results will be with a sustained and realistic program.

$\mathcal{T}$wenty five COMPTETITIONS AND DEFENSE TACTICS

I gained more confidence and shooting skills in a couple of seasons shooting IDPA (International Defense Pistol Association)[24] and IPSC (International Practical Shooting Confederation)[25] matches than I did in 20 years of shooting sporadically on my own. These matches helped me dramatically increase my gun handling skills, particularly drawing and shooting. It was not only the actual shooting at the matches that allowed me to advance my skills, but also the opportunity to talk to and learn from more experienced shooters.

IPSC and IDPA are fun sports for shooters of all levels of experience.

Both sports are considered action shooting competitions. They utilize multiple life-sized cardboard targets and steel plates, or 'poppers'. While each stage's requirements can vary, most require two shots to each paper target and the knocking over of the steel plates/poppers. Scores are calculated based on time and shot placement. Each cardboard target has zones inscribed in it to denote point zones. Shots in the center, or 'A', zone have no points added to the time. Shots in the outer zones have increasing points added to the time. The number of points varies by placement and by sport. The object of both sports is to have as low a score

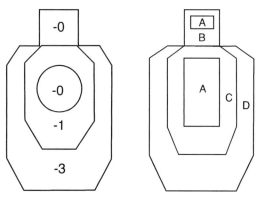

IDPA target on left and IPSC target on right.

as possible. I consider IDPA and IPSC matches to be great fun.

While you might think the sports are for good shooters only, quite the opposite is true. Both organizations encourage new shooters, and have different classes of capabilities and gun types so you are competing only with those in your class. The only requirement for shooting skills is that you are safe at all times.

IPSC was created as a 'practical' handgun sport, and has evolved greatly. There are categories for shooters of stock guns, called "production," as well as "revolver," "limited," "limited 10," and "open" classes. The latter allows ultra high-capacity magazines, red-dot sights, and compensators while the 'limited' class only allows high-capacity magazines, and some gun modifications. "Limited 10" restricts Limited guns to only 10 round magazines. "Production" and "revolver" categories are for stock guns, and the only modifications allowed are trigger jobs (smoothing out the triggger pull).

IDPA was formed because the IDPA founders felt that IPSC was going too high tech and was too 'competition' orientated, thereby no longer 'practical'. IDPA was created with 'carry' issues in mind to make the sport more reflective of realistic defensive situations. Guns and holsters are limited to 'carry guns' with no compensators, red dot sights, and competition modifications allowed. The stages are orientated towards protection scenarios such as holdups and attacks. Scoring is more shot placement orientated than time orientated, favoring better hits over speed. Try both sports and see which you like. With either one, it will be a great experience and you will have lots of fun.

While I highly recommend action competitions to increase skills and for fun, keep in mind that with a sport that is scored by time and bullet placement, it is inherent that in order to win, you must sacrifice tactical correctness. The skills that make you a winner in a match can get you killed on the street. Shooting sports are just that, sports, and should not be confused with tactical training.

If you do shoot competitively, you should modify your competition technique, and you must combine it with practical and realistic training sessions to retain and increase your street skills. There are several modifications that can be used to make sport shooting more realistic. They won't win you the match, but they may help you when it really counts.

IPSC is more of a speed orientated 'racing' sport that encourages speed over shot placement. You may actually get a better score if you get two fast 'C' shots than two slow 'A' shots. IDPA does emphasize shot placement over speed, but both sports permit poorly placed shots that would most likely be ineffective in a real defense situation. To maximize the quality of your shooting, keep shooting until you get nothing less than two 'A' hits. When I say a minimum of "two A" shots, I do mean minimum. Just because the stage requires two hits,

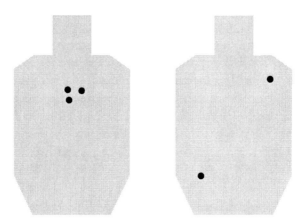

"A" shots (hits in critical areas) are more likely to be manstoppers than "C" and "D" shots (hits off to the sides).

it does not mean that you can't have more. You won't get extra points (and may even loose some if two is the maximum) and it will increase your time, but you will be reinforcing good defense tactics. Remember, don't shoot as fast as you can pull the trigger, shoot as fast as you can hit properly. You can't miss fast enough to win a gunfight.

Use the same concept on plates and pepper poppers. Think of the plates/poppers as attackers. If you face one popper, follow the popper down with your fire and don't stop shooting until it is lying down on the ground. Best practice on the street is to keep shooting until the threat stops — that is rarely just one shot. If you face several attackers

Treat poppers on the practice range and in competitions the same way you would treat an attacker on the street — keep shooting until they are down.

(plates/poppers), engage the closest one first (assuming all attackers pose the same threat, the closest should be engaged first) with one round. Hit or miss, continue with just one round for each popper until you have engaged them all, then repeat as often as necessary with one round each until they are all down. If they pose various threats, the target which presents the greatest threat (has the most deadly weapon or the assailant most ready to attack) should be shot first.

IDPA is better than IPSC for requiring proper use of cover; however, it is still not realistic enough for defense purposes. First of all, use cover at all possible times, even when not called for in the stage. Secondly, the competition rule is that at least 50% of your body needs to be concealed for it to be considered proper use of cover. If someone were actually shooting back, I don't think that you would want only half of your body protected. Expose only the parts you must in order to get your shot, and keep the rest of your body protected. Keep in mind that what you are hiding behind is more likely concealment, not cover. If you can, shoot from different locations and at diferent heights behind the cover/concealment to keep the attacker from knowing where you are and where you will be at your next shot.

IPSPA and IPSC matches require just 50% of your body to be behind cover. In reality, it is imperative to keep as much of your body protected as possible.

Threat scan at the end of each stage segment and end of the stage. Don't forget the 180 rule which requires you to keep the muzzle of your gun within a 180 degree arc of the starting line.

If you carry a 2-inch snub revolver and compete with a 5-inch custom 1911, you are not availing yourself of the opportunity to practice with what you carry. Some say that they can't shoot their snubby as well as their large frame gun. If that is the case, why carry something that you cannot shoot well? Consider either changing carry guns or practicing more with your carry gun. Regardless of what you carry, wear the holster and magazine holders that you carry and don't forget to use the same concealment garments that you normally wear.

IDPA requires the use of 'tactical reloads,' and 'magazine changes with retention' both requiring that the magazines be retained by the shooter after reloading. The 'tactical reload' also requires that the magazine change be done "at the gun', meaning that the spare magazine is drawn prior to the ejection of the partial magazine and both magazines are held in the same hand during the reload. You are not allowed to store the partial magazine in your pocket until the reload is complete in order to get your gun back into action as soon as possible forcing you to keep the ejected magazine in you hand as your try to reload.

The concept is that if you change magazines during a 'lull in the action' and the magazine that you eject still has one or more rounds in it, you should keep it. Checking to be sure you have a spare magazine before you eject a partial one is a good idea, however, holding the ejected magazine in the same hand as the fresh one during a reload is very cumbersome.

I don't know of a single street-wise tactical instructor that agrees with the concept of having both the ejected and fresh magazine in your hand during a reload for two reasons: First, it is very difficult to do in the best of situations, and is almost an impossibility to accomplish under the extreme stress of a lethal encounter. Secondly, in a real-life gunfight, every fraction of a second counts and you don't have time to fumble with an ejected magazine.

Retaining a partial magazine and keeping it your hand during a reload might be fine when you have plenty of time to execute a reload from behind cover. A 'lull in the action' may be available in a police or military operation where action takes place in stages and there are several members in an the assault team working together. However, there is mostly likely not going to be the luxury of time to do a tactical reload in the type of life and death scenario that a ordinary citizen would likely to be in. Generally, you're going to shoot until the attacker is down. Reload if empty, but if you still have bullets you should find better cover, if needed, cover your attacker, and threat scan for more attackers, and *only then* worry about refreshing your ammunition supply. Keep in mind, as soon as you remove the magazine from the gun, another previously unseen attacker may reveal himself. At that point, do you *really* want the magazine to be out of the gun? To aggravate matters even more, some guns won't fire without a magazine inserted!

You will find that top tennis players usually do not play racquetball. Although similar, the two racket sports are different, and playing one can negatively effect the other. Similar issues arise with shooting sports. While they are lot of fun and can dramatically increase your shooting skills, choose your goals carefully, discern how the sport can affect your defensive techniques, and modify appropriately.

Twenty Six ## AFTER THE CONFRONTATION WHAT NEXT?

Sneaking around the outside of a house at 3 A.M., the criminal sees and hears no signs that his chosen victims are awake. With a padded covering, he uses his elbow to break a basement window. Slipping inside, he makes his way up the stairs, stopping to pick up a small piece of 2x4 along the way. Hearing the glass break and noise downstairs, you gather your family to the master bedroom. Hiding behind concealment, a family member calls 911, while you get your weapon.

The criminal crosses the hallway towards your bedroom and you realize that he is heading right for you and your family. You instantly blind him with your flashlight and he obeys your order; **"DON'T MOVE. DROP THE WEAPON."**

Now what?

You have stopped the potential crime and have saved your family and yourself from the harm intended by the criminal — so far. Your subsequent actions will determine how safe you all remain.

If you confront a criminal you must be authoritative and create situation dominance.

If you had fatally shot the criminal, there would be no worry of impending violence, and your area of concern would shift to the legal ramifications of the shooting. But tonight, he's alive, scared, angry, and still very much a threat. Put yourself in the shoes of the now detained criminal. He has just been caught 'breaking and entering,' and who knows what other charges could apply. He had a weapon and was looking for, and expecting to find, sleeping victims. If someone breaks into a home knowing that there are people inside, you have to assume there would be no hesitation to commit acts of violence. Sum it up and you have a violent criminal, facing jail time, who is backed into a corner and looking for any way to escape at any cost — a very dangerous predicament for the good guy.

At this point, your job is to protect your family by creating and maintaining situational dominance over the criminal until the police arrive. While one chapter can't cover every possible contingency, this plan will outline an effective and accepted procedure for handling a single attacker. If you face multiple criminals, the approach is the same. Start with the one that poses the greatest threat, and keep them together so you can keep your eyes in the same place. If the criminal does not speak English, or pretends not to speak English, you will have to use exaggerated body movements to communicate. Keep your gun hand steady and be careful to keep the gun pointed at the criminal at all times so as to not give him a greater opportunity to attack.

The first thing that you have to remember is that while the following is a good plan of procedure, everything does not always go according to plan. The bad guy has his own ideas of how events should unfold, and may not be cooperative. He may lull you into a sense of control and strike when he thinks that you're not prepared or alert. He may simply refuse to obey you, or he may attack. He may pretend to be submissive or cooperative to get you to drop your guard. Always stay alert and be ready for the unexpected.

Now, let's get back to where we left off; The criminal is blinded by your tactical flashlight and you are holding him at gunpoint. His weapon has been dropped and he is awaiting your instructions. Keep your family at a safe distance so you can focus your full attention on the threat at hand.

To maintain dominance, keep your flashlight in his eyes to keep him blinded. Keep the room lights off, as the less ambient light there is, the less he will be able to see. If your flashlight starts to dim due to weakening batteries, you will be forced to turn on the room lights. (This is a great reason to change your flashlight's batteries regularly even if you have not used it.)

Before turning on the room lights, you need to gain further situational dominance by putting the attacker in a physical position that will be the most difficult from which to attack.

Distance is your friend. There is no tactical advantage by being close, only danger. If attacked, you can just as easily shoot him at 20 feet as you can at 5 feet. Up close, he has more advantages than you might realize. At close range, he can disarm you faster than you can pull the trigger. While that might sound hard to fathom, it has been proven true time after time. Action beats reaction. If a move is made to disarm you at close range, you must first perceive the movement, realize that it is an attempt to take your weapon, decide what your reaction will be, and only then fend off the gun grab. The longest part of that process is the perception of the movement and the determination of the threat. The attacker will be able to take the gun from your hands before your mind even perceives the danger.

Start by informing him in a very loud, deep, commanding voice: **"IF YOU MAKE ANY FAST MOVEMENTS, I WILL ASSUME THAT YOU ARE GOING TO ATTACK ME AND I WILL SHOOT YOU."** The next step is to order the him to lift his hands high above his head. Again, all of your commands need to be in a loud, deep, commanding voice. If this doesn't describe your everyday voice, this is another thing you should practice if you want to have it available when you need it. If he starts to move

Hands must be high above the head, not near the
shoulders to prohibit access to a hidden weapon.

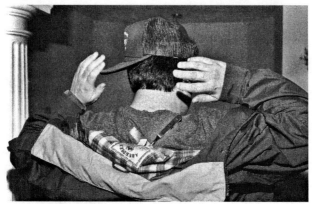

Note the weapon taped on his back

his hands anywhere else besides above his head, especially to the back of his head or behind his back, order him again to move them above his head. Continued motion in a direction other than ordered is a sure sign that he is going for a hidden weapon.

If his weapon or anything else that can be used as a weapon is near his feet, order him to **"SLOWLY, KICK YOUR WEAPON (or whatever object is close) TO YOUR LEFT (OR RIGHT) SIDE.** Have it kicked in a direction that will be far from his reach but also not near you. You don't want to pick the weapon up, as it diverts your attention from the criminal, ties up one hand, and may disturb the criminal's fingerprints or other forensic evidence. Also, bending over will eliminate your position of dominance and give the criminal a perfect opportunity to attack. You don't want it at your feet either, because you don't want to trip over it, nor do you want to be looking down to avoid tripping over it when you move. Alternatively, you may order him to **"BACK AWAY FROM THE WEAPON"** (and away from you and your family).

Once his hands are in the proper position, the next order should be **"SLOWLY, GET ON YOUR KNEES"**. Order him to then walk on his knees with his hands high above his head to a place that is large enough for him to lay down and does not block you from reaching your family, the telephone and the door, and is also not near any potential weapons. From this point on the criminal should never be allowed to stand again. If you need to move him again for any reason, he should do so on his knees or from a stomach crawl.

Command the perpetrator to his knees to limit his movements.

Get him on the floor by ordering him to **"SLOWLY LAY DOWN ON THE FLOOR."** The final position changes are designed to greatly slow down his ability to get up and attack: **"SPREAD YOUR ARMS OUT TO YOUR SIDES AND FACE THE PALMS OF YOUR HANDS UP."** When completed, the next order should be: **"TURN YOUR AHEAD AWAY FROM ME AND LAY YOUR FACE FLAT AGAINST THE FLOOR."**

The final order is; **"CROSS YOUR LEGS AT THE ANKLES."**

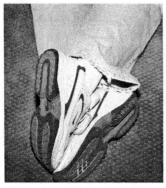

Feet should be crossed to make getting up more difficult.

The final position has the assailant face down, looking away from you, arms spread with palms upward, and feet crossed.

It is now time to remind him not to move; **"IF YOU MAKE ANY FAST MOVEMENTS, I WILL ASSUME THAT YOU ARE GOING TO ATTACK ME AND I WILL SHOOT YOU."**

If you have to divert your eyes or move to get the phone, have him crawl on his belly in a direction so you don't have to take your eyes off him. Whatever you have to do, never lower your guard or your weapon, and keep your distance. Never try to cuff or tie up the suspect because that would open you up for a disarm or attack. Remember, distance is your friend.

It is best to have a family member stay on the phone with the police throughout the entire incident to keep them apprised. If the police are still on the line, inform them of the fact that you are now holding the bad guy on the floor at gunpoint. If the call was disconnected already, call the police again and tell them your current situation. (It is important for the police to get an update so that they know that the good guy is the person who is holding the gun.) If there was not time to make a call to the police previously, now is the time, since the criminal is in the most awkward physical position possible.

Any time that you call 911, give your address right away, and give it again to be sure they have it. Not all 911 systems display the address automatically. It is best to give the address first because if you get cut off for any reason, the police will at least know where you are and that you are in danger. Next, give them your name and tell them that you are at home, holding at gunpoint a criminal who just broke into your home. At this time repeat the warning to the criminal: **"IF YOU MAKE ANY FAST MOVEMENTS, I WILL ASSUME THAT YOU ARE GOING TO ATTACK ME AND I WILL SHOOT YOU."** Do this again while on the phone with the police in order to get your warning recorded by the police's phone recording system. If you have to shoot to defend yourself, the tape could go a long way in your defense.

Describe yourself to the police, including what you are wearing. Describe the criminal and what he is wearing. Be simple, be specific, and make a special effort to speak slowly and clearly. Remember that you will be under tremendous stress and may mumble, slur, or speak so quickly that the police could have trouble understanding. Tell them where you are in the house and how to get there from the main door. If a mature member of your family can meet the police at the door without having to walk near the criminal, have them open the door for the officer(s) and give them a description of what is happening. The family member needs to inform the officer who you are and what you look like so there is no mistake as to who the criminal is. If you are alone or unable to open the door safely, tell the 911 operator that you "give permission for the officer(s) to break the door in order to enter" because you do not want to take your eyes off the criminal for even a second.

Once the police are within earshot, advise them that you are the homeowner and the person on the floor broke into your home (with a weapon, if that is the case). Once the police arrive, **they are in charge and you must follow the officers' orders exactly and immediately.** Picture the situation from their perspective: They come into a home and find someone on the floor at gunpoint. Who looks like the one who is threatening the life of another? Make sure the police know who the good guy is.

A caged animal is the most dangerous kind. The criminal knows he's going to jail and may feel he has nothing to loose. You may have disarmed the attacker, but that does not render him benign. These procedures will help you maintain control until the police arrive.

Twenty Seven — CONSEQUENCES OF A SHOOTING

It is said that the more you know about gun fighting, the less you want to be involved in one. The emotional and legal torment that will follow a shooting is testament to that declaration. Before you pull the trigger, know what you're in for afterwards.

If you are involved in a situation that requires the use of lethal force, you need to have a thorough understanding of what will happen to you psychologically, physiologically, and legally. If you are in the unfortunate position of having been forced to defend yourself or a loved one, this knowledge will help you overcome the mental and physical effects, and will assist you in navigating the myriad of legal issues and situations in which you may find yourself.

Regardless of whether you were within your rights to use lethal force or not, understand this: you have just committed the most heinous act a human being can perform — you have injured or killed another human being. There will be effects on your mind and body, the extent of which will vary greatly from person to person.

You may feel a range of emotions running from guilt to elation. I say "may," because every situation is different, and everyone reacts differently. It is possible to feel a small dose of opposing emotions, or a lot of just one. The emotions may appear immediately or later — even much later in time. Duration may be short for some people and longer for others.

Since you have probably spent your entire life accommodating others rather than doing them harm, you may feel guilt for your actions. Guilt, like other emotions, is common when someone is involved in a shooting, even a justified shooting. You need to realize that while you did commit the act, it was *the action of the perpetrator that caused your action.* The attacker is the guilty party. To affirm yourself and justify your actions, you will need to understand that you are not the one who attacked another person. You were right to protect yourself. You have saved your life or that of someone else. You are the good person.

One of the most immediate reactions might be that of elation — an extreme happiness at surviving a life-threatening situation. It may seem wrong to feel happy about the death or injury of another, but there is nothing immoral in applauding your own survival.

You may feel repulsion, manifested in the form of fainting, vomiting, and nausea at both the act and the bloody results. For a period of time you may feel consumed with self-doubt. Did I really need to shoot? Was there anything else that I could have done?

Finally, after those emotions have run their course, you will find rationalization, vindication, and finally, acceptance. Again, this acceptance comes from the knowledge that you needed to do what you did, and that you were right in doing it.

The best way to overcome the emotional effects of violence is through counseling. Talking with a professional, and/or other people who have also survived similar encounters, is the best therapy. Due to the hazards of the job, police officers have a strong support group of fellow officers who have faced the ugly reality of violence. The average citizen not only does not have this built-in support, but may actually experience just the opposite — scorn from others. Personal emotions, combined with contempt from the public in which they wrongly blame the victim, can extend and deepen the emotional consequences. It is important to seek out the help of a social worker, psychologist, clergy, friends and family to help overcome the onslaught of emotions.

Legal Aftermath

The concept of innocent until proven guilty will seemingly be turned on its head if you are involved in a shooting. You will be handcuffed. You will be arrested. You will be charged. All of the preceding will most likely occur even if you were acting in your own defense.

When the police arrive, say nothing. You will be in a complete state of shock. You may be an emotional wreck due to extreme adrenaline release and other Body Alarm Reactions. Your recollection of the events may not be clear. The timetable of the attack may be distorted, and you are very likely to inadvertently say something that will get you in deep trouble.

Inform the responding officers that the perpetrator attacked you and tried to injure or kill you, and that you had to defend yourself. Advise them that you intend to cooperate fully, but wish to seek counsel with an attorney before making a statement. Say nothing more at this point. You have a constitutional right to an attorney, and this will in no way imply guilt. If the police indicate that they need an immediate statement from you for the investigation, it is not true, so advise them again that you wish to consult your attorney before making any statement.

Keep in mind that the police officers that you speak with are not your friends. No matter how friendly or sympathetic they seem, their job is not to keep you out of trouble, but to assign blame. As the Miranda Rights state: "Anything that you say or do will be used against you." Once you say something, it can never be erased. The grand jury and jury will be told every damaging word you say. Give yourself time to calm down, collect your thoughts, and get good legal advice.

It is imperative to engage an attorney who is experienced in defense of cases that involve use of lethal force. The best attorneys are the ones who have successfully defended police officers that were involved in a shooting. Contact the local police union to find out which attorneys they use.

Well before you are involved in a shooting, it is a good idea to interview and choose an attorney. You never know when you will need one, and being behind bars will limit your ability to shop around. It is best to keep your attorney's name, office and home phone numbers with you at all times.

When interviewing attorneys, find out what types of lethal force cases they have been involved in, and what types of defenses were mounted. Be sure to find an attorney that believes in, and uses, an **affirmative defense.** An affirmative defense states that you did commit the act, but it was justified.

One famous case had the defending attorney ignore the affirmative defense, and instead had the defendant testify that the shooting was an accident because his gun went off unintentionally. What made the defendant's jail sentence so sad and unnecessary was that his actions were, in fact, truly justified. Had he testified that he purposefully shot the perpetrator and articulated the reasons why he felt that his life was in danger, the outcome of the verdict would probably have been in his favor.

Twenty Eight

SAFE
STORAGE

Safe For Who?...You?... Your Children?
Or, Safe For The Criminal?

Safe storage of weapons is a delicate topic that teeters between the balance of security and safety. Guns, knives, and pepper spray need to be accessed quickly in order to be useful for defense, yet it is essential that they be kept out of the hands of children, thieves, and other unauthorized people. The biggest argument against 'safe storage' laws that require guns to be secured against unauthorized use, is that the same security device that prevents children from playing with guns, also prevents the owner from using the gun for defense. A gun with a trigger lock is just a hunk of metal.

I categorize storage devices into long-term storage and quick action security. While many manufacturers portray their products to be quick action, the reality is that they don't always work quickly enough and reliable enough to be used for self-defense.

A full-sized safe is a great way to store firearms for the long-term. I recommend spending a little extra to get the fire protection option. Make sure you bolt the safe down in as many places as possible. While it might seem impossible for someone to break in and steal a 600-pound safe, keep in mind that what can be carried in, can be carried out. Today's safes offer entry through a standard dial, electronic keypad, and even fingerprint scan devices. Some models of keypads are even removable to keep people from fumbling with them. Be a smart shopper — you can spend a lot of money on gadgets that may really not be worth the cost. It's a good idea to talk to a safe retailer to find out what companies make good safes, and what options are really worth the extra cost.

If you are planning on having just one or two handguns, size of the safe is not an issue. From the office supply store to safe retailers, small safes can be found at a large number of quality (and price) levels. If you are a gun enthusiast like myself, buy a safe big enough to house the anticipated size of your collection years into the future. Regardless of the size, make sure you use an electric drying device to keep the air inside your safe dry and your guns free of rust.

While a high-quality safe offers the best protection, gun

cabinets and low-cost safes are far better than nothing. My first gun safe was a $300 model that I purchased at a department store. Bolted into the cement floor and wall, it's good enough to keep my son, visitors, and most amateur thieves away.

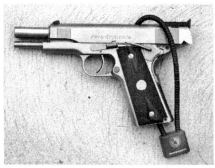

Three examples of gun locks.

I am amazed at the number of products on the market to lock up firearms. From the usual trigger locks to magazine locks, barrel locks, and other devices, each one proclaims itself as the better mousetrap. Regardless of how advanced one such lock is over another, each has a shared feature: the need to use a key, turn a dial or enter a code, and that's where the problem lies.

With all key locks, the question is: Will you be able to locate your key ring at one location in your house, run to the location where your gun is stored, select the right key, insert a tiny key into a tiny hole, and deactivate the locking mechanism before a criminal can reach you? The answer is probably not. If trigger locks are so effective and quick, why don't police use them in their holsters?

"Quick action" safes are designed to be opened quickly usually using a keypad or some kind of quick combination mechanism. While combination locks and push buttons eliminate the need for a key, you still need to get to your safe, remember your combination, press the keys in the proper order and with the proper amount of pressure, in the proper amount of time. I find that many electrical and mechanical locks are sensitive to the amount of pressure applied and the speed in which the code is entered. Too fast or too slow, it may not work.

Quick action safe (Rifle Locker) mounted in a closet wall.

The same thing can happen if you hit the keypad too hard or too soft. Getting all that right while you heart is beating twice normal and your hands are shaking is not easy.

I recently had the opportunity to test out two biometric safes that utilize fingerprint scanning devices to access the safe. While I hold high hopes for this technology, it does not appear ready for emergency use at this time.

I found the fingerprint reading device too sensitive to how much pressure is placed against the screen, the exact placement of the finger, and the finger print itself. After doing some heavy work and roughing up the skin on my finger, I found that the scanner would read my fingerprint only about 1 out of 5 times. Sometimes it did read the print, but it took far too long. Regardless of why it didn't work, I would not rely on the technology at this time for something that your life depends on. Biometric technology will evolve and it may become a viable solution in the future.

Ever-increasing numbers of liability suits have led some gun manufactures to include gun locks that are built right into the gun. Unfortunately, to date, they have not been perfectly reliable. I have heard more than one story of a gun that froze because the internal safety malfunctioned. The adage of the more moving parts, the more chance there is of a breakdown, holds true. I keep away from all guns with internal locks because with all life saving devices, additional chances of malfunction are unacceptable.

Unfortunately, safe storage is an area of gun ownership where there is no easy solution — both in relation to what level of security is required, as well as to the choice of safety devices themselves. Safe storage has been, and will always be, a compromise.

My recommendation is to look at as many products as you can and try them in the store. If you find one that you like, make sure that there is a return policy, and test it at home the way you would use it for real. Don't just set it and forget it, use it for an extended time and see how well it works. I like to place the safe where it will actually be used and run access drills in real time, at full speed. I will actually run in from another room, kneel down, or get into whatever position necessary, and try to open the safe. I also test and train in the dark because if I would need retrieve a weapon for real, I would access the in the dark to keep the tactical advantage.

Try Entering the codes at different speeds, and pressing the buttons at different angles with different levels of pressure. Do this many times over a few days to see if the results change. I have found several safes that seemed good, but after extended practice, they proved to be less than reliable. Keep in mind, if there is a problem, it might not be the safe, it could be that it just requires more practice on your part. Like everything else, you need to keep up on your practice of opening your safe so if an emergency does occur, you will be ready.

Twenty Nine BACK-UP GUNS AND OTHER SAFETY TOOLS

The best retort I have heard when someone was asked 'Why do you carry three guns?' was "because I thought four would be ostentatious".

While it may seem overboard, in reality, there are several good reasons for carrying one or more back-up guns. First, and foremost, is simply as a back-up. It is not a good time for a breakdown or jam when your life is in imminent danger. While breakage or a jam may be unlikely, you **need** to have an alternative if your life depends on a mechanical device. Guns, like every other mechanical device, do break, and every owner of a semi-auto knows that they can and do jam. Back-up guns are no different than a spare tire in the trunk of your car, or carrying a second parachute when skydiving.

Additionally, back-up guns can be utilized in lieu of a reload, often called a 'New York reload'. In the event that your dominant hand is injured or occupied, your support hand may be able to reach the back-up gun more easily than your primary gun. Having a backup also allows you to hand a gun to someone else (if trained) if need be.

Back-up guns tend to be smaller than primary guns, but be sure they are still in an effective caliber. With all of the diminutive guns available today in good calibers, there is no need to carry a substandard caliber. For consistency, keep the trigger and safety systems the same if possible. If you carry a double action with no external safety for your main gun, don't carry a gun with an external safety for a backup. If possible, get a smaller version of your primary gun, such as a Glock 26 as a back-up to a Glock 17. The operation will be the same, and the spare magazines will operate in both guns. Some people like a revolver as a back-up, because if they have to give it to someone, they can use it instinctively without having to worry about safeties and the like.

Carry locations for back-ups tend to be a little difficult because, by definition, the primary gun occupies the best location. Support-side belt, pockets, waist packs, ankle holsters and some deep concealment locations make for good back-up carry locations. See the chapter on concealed carry and alternative methods for more information.

The person that carries more than one gun is not paranoid, but is prepared.

Spare Ammunition

There are a few other items that should be carried as well — spare ammunition tops the list. For a semi-auto, you should carry a least one extra magazine, for two reasons: 1. Extra ammunition if you run out and 2. In case of a jam, gun malfunction, or a bad round, changing the magazine is often the first thing to do to fix the problem. For a revolver, while it is most efficient to carry a speed

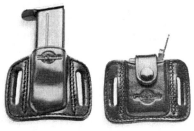

Magazine holder and speed strip carrier by Mitch Rosen.

loader, it is not often practical under concealed carry conditions. Putting the loader is a pocket or waist pack will work if you can get to it fast enough. With a speed loader or magazine, make sure they stay clean. Pockets, waist packs, and similar methods tend to collect dust and dirt. If you can't find a good location for a speed loader, the next best alternative is a speed strip, which allows you to load two bullets at a time off a rubber strip. You can buy speed strip carriers to wear on your belt. Another alternative is a dump pouch, which, as its name states, dumps the rounds into your hand at once. These can also be worn on your belt, but tend to be awkward because all of the cartridges are in your hand at the same time.

Knives

A folding knife can serve both as a back-up, and for other utility purposes. Personally, to keep my knives as sharp as possible, I don't use them to cut anything — they are strictly reserved for protection. I keep a small knife on my key ring for utility use. A knife also serves as a good primary defensive weapon in locations where were the law may prohibit the carry of firearms, but allows pocket knives.

3 to 5-inch blade length is ideal for personal defense, but the shorter the blade, the better it could look to a jury. It is imperative to check state and local laws to find out if knives are legal to carry and conceal, and if so, what kind and what size. As far as blade style, do not use serrated, partially serrated, or 'mean' looking blades — plain blades cut just as well and, again, look far better to the jury. Likewise, juries don't like knives that have 'evil' names inscribed it in them like 'Terminator' or 'Annihilator'. Even the handle color could be important — a pink-handled knife cuts just as

well as the same knife with a "tactical black" handle, but somehow looks "less offensive" to much of the general public from which your jury could be drawn.

We are in a 'golden age' of knives, as there are lots of companies that make lots of good quality knives. Features to consider are clip or non-clip, right or left hand, and non-slip handles. These days, you don't need to spend $200 to get a quality knife — $50 will get you a pretty good knife. If you spend much less than that, you will get what you paid for.

Folding knives come in many sizes and styles. In choosing a knife, the first two decisions should be the opening mechanism and the locking mechanism.

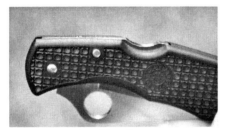

Lockback.

Liner lock.

Piston Lock.

Locking mechanisms are utilized to keep the blade open during use. Locking designs include the traditional lockback, a spring-driven tang lock, and a liner lock. The lockback is held open by spring-loaded armature and is most commonly used. With the tang lock design, a spring pressures a locking piston into the blade's tang. A liner lock is an armature that slides over from the 'lining' of the internal frame to behind the tang to keep the blade from closing. The liner lock and tang lock designs have the least tension making them the easiest to open.

Be sure you get a knife that can be opened one-handed, and with either hand. One hand opening mechanisms include, for the most part, stud, or hole designs. The hole design is simply a hole in the blade, about the size of a dime, in which you place your thumb in order to rotate the blade open. By design they work with either hand. The stud design incorporates a small protrusion on the blade that you place your thumb against to push open. To open with either hand, the knife needs to have a double-sided stud.

Examples of hole and stud designs.

I prefer a design that allows a somewhat looser blade hinge (liner lock or tang) allowing the blade to be flicked opened by a quick, downward movement of the wrist. To open a knife with your thumb requires specific placement of the hand and thumb to be able to open the blade. If you don't get a proper grip in the right location, you will have to shift your grip to be able to open the knife. If your knife will flick open, the grip placement will not be as critical. The opening of liner lock or tang lock knife by a flick of your wrist is not to be confused with the use of a 'gravity knife', which are widely illegal. While outlawed in many states, statues do not actually define what constitutes a gravity knife. Knife experts define a gravity knife as a knife, with a blade, that when properly positioned, can be opened by the force of gravity exclusively. It is generally held that opening a liner or tang lock knife with a flick of the wrist is considered the use of inertia, not gravity, since the blade will not open with the force of gravity alone, but will only open when acted upon with a thrusting motion. In many jurisdictions there is little or no case law in this area, so is highly speculative as to whether a knife that can be opened by a flick of the wrist may be considered a gravity knife or not. As with all legal issues, it is imperative to check the laws in your state.

No matter what knife you decide to carry, I strongly suggest you take a class on proper knife techniques to learn about safety, carry issues, proper deployment and get the 'tricks of the trade'.

Cell Phone

Whether you carry a gun or not, for safety, an absolute must for everyone is a cell phone. Cell phones are essential to call for help and to get information wherever you are. You do not need to get a full calling plan and spend a lot of money. Many cell phone companies have plans that do not require credit checks or long term contracts. Pay-as-you-go cellular service is very cost effective if you use the phone only for emergencies. In many areas, 911 works for free even if you do not have an active cell phone account.

Pepper Spray

Pepper spray is a good defensive alternative when lethal force is not applicable. Made with the oil of cayenne peppers, pepper spray is used to slow down an attacker by stinging the eyes and skin. While non-lethal, being sprayed in the face with it is painful and may temporarily disable an attacker, offering you extra time to escape or defend yourself.

Pepper spray comes in a variety of strengths, formulations, sizes, and packaging and can be carried in a pocket, in a purse, or on a belt. I suggest the standard one to two ounce container with a flip-top or other safety device. Found on the Internet and at most gun stores, good brands include 'Sabre' manufactured by Security Equipment Corporation, and 'Guardian' by Guardian Protective Devices. Check with your local police department to see if you need a permit to purchase and/or carry pepper spray. While it may not be required by your local laws, I highly recommend taking a class in its proper use.

Tactical Flashlight

A good tactical flashlight can help save your life. Much brighter than an ordinary flashlight, a tactical flashlight (60 lumens or more) can be used by flashing it in an attacker's eyes to startle and/or cause temporary blindness, to give you some extra time to escape

SureFire tactical flashlight.

or defend yourself. These lights are also useful for scanning dark areas and long distances at night. Until recently, these lights were only used by law enforcement, but they offer benefits for everyone. Found at many types of retailers, recommended brands include: 'SureFire'[26], 'Streamlight'[27], and 'Pelican'[28].

Blade-Tech magazine and flashlight carrier.

SureFire flashlight with rifle/shotgun mount and pressure pad.

Insight Technology's M3 light rail mounted to a H&K USP.

Over the shoulder, near the cheek is one method to use a handheld tactical flashlight.

For shotguns and rifles, use a mounted light with a momentary contact pressure pad on the forestock. It is important to be able to turn the light on and off as needed rather than have it on all the time, which can quickly drain the batteries, and may give away your position. The drawbacks of a weapon-mounted light are twofold. 1. You have to point a loaded weapon at someone in order to illuminate them. (not only dangerous, but could be considered a felony) 2. You are unable to point your weapon at one location and the light at another. With long guns, there are not many alternatives to weapon-mounted lights since it takes two hands to control them.

There are several techniques for using a light with a handgun. Many guns manufactured these days feature mounting rails for flashlights and lasers, but then you have the same functional drawbacks as the long guns. Additionally, depending on the light design and length of your fingers, you may need your support hand to activate the switch.

Another method is to carry a tactical light separately. This way you don't have to worry about trying to find a new holster to fit a gun/light combination, and your light holding techniques can be more flexible and adaptable to the situation.

The biggest tactical advantages of a hand-held light are that you can illuminate one subject while pointing the gun at another, and that it eliminates the need to point a loaded gun at someone in order to illuminate them. Additional, bad guys often automatically shoot towards the light, thinking that the person is directly behind it. Holding the light off to the side tends to frustrate the assailant's efforts.

There are lots of books and magazine articles that cover commonly used flashlight techniques. Like everything else, each technique has its advantages and disadvantages. Try them all and see what works for you. When testing, don't just test them standing still. Test them while scanning, using multiple targets, shooting around cover, and running.

Reading this, you are probably asking, "How do I carry all of this stuff?" To be honest, it is not easy and with certain dress requirements, particularity work dress requirements, it may not be possible to carry everything. If you are limited to what you can carry, prioritize what you may need, and carry what you can. While traveling, waist packs can hold a lot of safety tools. You can also carry some items in a cell phone case or small camera case on your belt. Just as you would a gun and holster, practice retrieving and utilizing all of your safety tools. Be thoughtful as to what, where, and how you carry, as you will never really know what you will need or when you will need it until the time comes. Then it is too late to have guessed wrong.

Thirty   # RULES FOR
A GUNFIGHT

*I came across this list as an anonymous posting floating around
the Internet. This rewrite makes it more realistic and useful.*

- If you know you are heading to a gunfight, **DON'T GO**.

- If you have no choice, and the gunfight is brought to you, have
a gun — preferably two. Have lots of ammunition. Rifles
and shotguns are better than handguns unless in confined
places like a doorway or hallway.

- Be courteous to everyone, drop your guard for no one.

- Be polite. Be professional. But, realize that everyone you meet
(or don't see) can present a threat. Immediately formulate a
plan to neutralize every threat you encounter.

- Have a back-up plan, because the first probably won't work.

- Use a gun that works flawlessly **every time** with your carry
ammunition.

- Act quickly and decisively, but don't act too soon or
overreact.

- Use cover

- Use cover

- Use cover

- Anything worth shooting is worth shooting more than once.
Don't stop shooting until the threat has stopped.

- A slow hit is better than a fast miss.

- Realize that every shot you fire hits somewhere. A miss
on your attacker may hit an innocent. Take bystanders and
backstops into account.

- A hit with a small caliber is better than a miss with a .45

- Forget Weaver. If your shooting stance is proper, you are not moving fast enough or using cover correctly.

- Move away from your attacker. Distance is your friend. (Lateral and diagonal movements are best.)

- In ten years, nobody will remember the details of caliber, stance, or tactics. They will only remember who lived.

- If you are not shooting, you should be communicating, reloading, and/or running.

- Win at any cost (except harm to innocents). There is no such thing as a fair fight. Somebody will have the advantage. Make sure it's you.

- Flank your adversary when possible. Protect your own flanks.

- Watch the hands. Eyes might be the windows to the soul, but hands kill. (In God we trust. Everyone else, keep your hands where I can see them.)

- After you stop the assailant, scan for others. Always threat scan 360 degrees.

- When searching for bad guys, look for exposed parts of the body (foot, hand, etc.), not just a full body.

- The sooner the fight ends, the less shot you will get.

Thirty One   # GUN
CONTROL

> *"A well regulated population,*
> *being necessary to the security of a police state,*
> *the right of the government to register and*
> *ban arms shall not be infringed."*
> *- apocryphal*

Take it from someone that used to ignore politics and gun control. It is **imperative** that every gun owner stays abreast of national and local gun legislation and do everything possible to stop gun control. If not, one by one, as history shows, we **will** lose all of our rights.

Politics

I remember laughing at the NRA, back in 1993, for coming out against the proposed assault weapons ban. How, in their right minds, could they come out against the ownership by private citizens of 'weapons of war'? At the time, I had no idea that my mind was fogged with the deception and deceit of the liberals.

Since my days of naiveté, I have become very politically aware and very concerned with gun control issues and their consequences. Most importantly, I became aware of how the lack of understanding on the part of voters and politicians can have drastically negative effects.

Many politicians lie. Yes, really! Gun control is one of their favorite follies. They twist the facts, spin the research, and spit it back out in a form totally unrecognizable from the truth. The media eats it up and disperses mountains of fabrications on nearly every radio station, web page, magazine and newspaper imaginable keeping the average citizen from understanding the true issues.

I consider gun control to be the perfect integrity test for politicians. All evidence from across the country and around the world points to the facts that disarming potential victims increases crime, and that guns in the hands of law-abiding citizens decreases crime. Yet, most of the Democrats (and far too many Republicans) spurn logic and promote gun control. Why? Simply put: votes.

Gun control is nothing more than a knee-jerk reaction to garner votes. Not only does gun control not work to reduce crime and accidents, it actually has the opposite effect. The politicians have two choices: do what is right for the country in order to control crime and protect its citizens or, pass gun control in order to garner votes, and the money and power that flow from those votes. When politicians choose votes over doing what is right, they fail the integrity test.

Media

I have been at news-making events. I have created news-making events. When I have read about them in the paper, I shook my head and asked myself, "How is it possible that the reporter and I were at the same event?" The media, what is supposed to be a bastion of truth, twist, distort, and lie to fit their own agenda. What is really scary is that if the media can't get a *simple* story right, what makes us believe that they can get a complicated story correct?

In the spring of 2003, CNN was forced to recant their story on the need to replace the expiring assault weapons ban, by totally fabricating a story about the dangers to society by so-called 'assault weapons".[29]

CNN attempted to illustrate how dangerous "assault weapons" were by comparing the results of a police officer firing a "banned assault rifle" and a non-banned, but similar, rifle, into a cinderblock. The first demonstration, with a non-banned, semi-automatic AK47 rifle showed no apparent damage. The second demonstration, using the so-called 'banned version of the same AK47' weapon, demolished the cinderblock. CNN asserted this as proof that "assault weapons" are more powerful and more dangerous than ordinary rifles, and therefore should be banned.

One problem was that the second weapon used in the demonstration was a fully automatic AK47, which isn't even part of the "assault weapon" ban because fully automatic weapons have been restricted since 1934. Most alarming, and what should be criminal, was the fact that in the first demonstration, the police officer purposely fired into the ground so as to not break the cinderblock and deceive the audience.

If that was not enough, they then went on mislead viewers on the power of "assault weapons" by showing an AK47 round piercing a bulletproof vest. They somehow forgot to mention that the vest in question was designed to stop only handgun rounds.

Thank the NRA for outing CNN on their outright deceptions and forcing them to recant their story. While the public relations damage was already done, at least CNN had to eat crow and lose credibility.

If the news media finds it acceptable to not only mislead, but to lie outright and fabricate their own 'facts', why should we trust **anything** coming from them?

For these reasons, it is incumbent upon each of us, regardless of the subject, to turn off the pundits, do our own research, and form our own opinions. If we, as gun owners, don't learn the facts and stand up for our rights, nobody will do it for us.

Here are just a few of the real "facts" of gun control:

Myth: Gun Control Reduces Crime

The definition of a criminal is someone who does not follow laws. That being the case, how will a law stop a criminal? Currently, there are more than 22,000[30] gun laws at the city, county, state, and federal level. If gun control laws worked, then we should already be free of crime.

John Lott, in his book, "More Guns, Less Crime"[31] proved that as gun ownership increases, crime decreases, and when gun control is increased, crime increases as well. Its common sense: if criminals fear their victims, there will be less crime. An armed victim is a criminal's only real deterrent.

In 1976, Washington, D.C. enacted one of the most restrictive gun control measures in the country. Since then, D.C.'s murder rate rose 134% while the nation's murder rate dropped 2%[32].

Maryland proudly claims to have the toughest gun control laws in the country. What doesn't make it into the promotional brochures is that they also rank #1 in robberies and #4 in both violent crime and murder.[33]

Fully twenty percent of U.S. homicides occur in four cities with just six percent of the population — New York, Chicago, Detroit, and Washington, D.C. — and each has a virtual prohibition on private handguns.[34]

Fact: Guns Stop Crime

Law-abiding citizens use firearms to stop crimes about 2.5 million times every year — or about 6,850 times a day.[35]

In 1979, the Carter Justice Department found that of more than 32,000 attempted rapes, 32% were actually committed. But when a woman was armed with a gun or knife, only 3% of the attempted rapes were actually successful.[36]

A U.S. Department of Justice study[37] concluded that:

- 60% of felons polled agreed that "a criminal is not going to mess around with a victim he knows is armed with a gun."

- 74% of felons polled agreed that "one reason burglars avoid houses when people are at home is that they fear being shot during the crime."

- 57% of felons polled agreed that "criminals are more worried about meeting an armed victim than they are about running into the police."

Citizens shoot and kill at least twice as many criminals as police do every year.[38] "Only 2% of civilian shootings involved an innocent person mistakenly identified as a criminal. The 'error rate' for the police, however, was 11%, more than five times as high."[39]

Assault Weapons

In reality, there is no such thing as an "assault weapon". It is a phrase invented by, and added to the English vernacular by the gun grabbers. Why did they invent their own language to describe their folly? Because if they had told the truth and simply called them "Guns that some people think look mean and scary but are no different, nor more powerful than other guns", they would have been laughed out of Congress.

The Violence Policy Center, a leading promoter of the "assault weapons" ban and one of the most extreme anti-gun organizations in existence, was so bold as to put their deceitful intentions in writing: *"The semi-automatic weapons' menacing looks, coupled with the public's confusion over fully automatic machine guns versus semi-automatic assault weapons — anything that looks like a machine gun is assumed to be a machine gun — can only increase that chance of public support for restrictions on these weapons."* [40]

What they said is that the public's lack of knowledge, and inability to tell the difference between real machine guns and rifles that simply look 'scary' will afford the ability to fool the public into supporting a ban against them. Sadly, their strategy not only worked on the public, but on politicians as well.

Title XI of the Federal Violent Crime Control Act of 1994, known to gun owners as the "assault weapon ban", banned the future manufacturing of so-called "assault weapons" and magazines with a capacity of over ten rounds. The bill defined an "assault weapon" as a semi-automatic rifle that has three or more "evil features". These evil features included: detachable magazine, pistol grip, folding or telescopic stock, bayonet mount, flash suppressor or threaded barrel, and grenade launcher. It also banned future manufacturing of magazines that held more than ten rounds.

Can anyone present a legitimate argument as to how adding a pistol grip makes a gun more deadly or dangerous? Will stopping the sale of rifles with bayonet mounts reduce the recent rash of drive-by bayonetings? How is it that one rifle that accepts detachable magazines should be banned, but other rifles in the same caliber that accepts detachable magazines are different, and should not be?

In actuality, the ban was based on cosmetics and ignorant fear rather than any legitimate sounding reason such as lethality or function. There are many other semi-auto firearms, that were not banned, that fired the same exact cartridges with the same exact bullets, also from detachable magazines. A perfect example is the AR-15, 'military looking' firearm with black synthetic stock compared to the Ruger Mini 14 which has a more conventional styling with pretty, "traditional" wooden stock. Both are gas-operated semi-automatic .223 rifles, and the only real difference is the look of the AR-15 with its black plastic stock and furniture.

Ruger Mini 14 semi-auto .223 rifle with "pretty" wood stock.

Les Baer AR15 semi-auto .223 rifle with "scary" black stock.

The new mantra of the gun grabbers is that "assault weapons" are the weapon of choice for criminals — again, not true. It has been proven that these type of firearms are only very rarely used in violent crimes (less than 0.25%)[41]

The gun grabbers ask "Why would anyone want to own a 'mean looking' gun like that?" First of all, looks don't matter, only function matters. Secondly, the rifle that the liars deemed to be scary are reliable, easy to shoot, fun to shoot, accurate, and have lots of accessories available making them great for both sport and defense. So the real question is "Why would anyone *not* want to own one?"

The "assault weapon" ban also included a ban on the manufacture of magazines that hold an excess of 10 rounds. It seems that the politicians feel that law-abiding citizens can be responsible with ten rounds of ammunition in their guns, but will turn into homicidal maniacs if given eleven rounds. Police are excused from this limitation and can carry any capacity magazine their department chooses. What I find so interesting is that police, who work in groups and have back-up available, are allowed to have larger capacity magazines, but law-abiding citizens that must defend themselves alone, are limited in how much ammunition they can have in their gun.

By law, the "assault weapons" ban was designed to expire after a ten-year period and it did so in September 2004. Fortunately, in one of the greatest victories in fighting gun control, it was not renewed at the time of expiration. However, it can be replaced at any time in the future by a similar if not more restrictive ban. Not satisfied with reinstating the previous ban, in 2004 the gun grabbers filed a bill in Congress that, if passed, would have not only continue the previous ban, but would also ban millions of additional guns. The proposed bill would ban every semi-automatic shotgun or rifle that the U.S. Attorney General decides isn't "sporting," (which means that we could not buy them for defense or sport) and would even ban the rifles most popular for marksmanship competitions: the Colt AR-15 and the M1 "Garand." With the sunsetting of the federal law, many states have passed similar bills, again making these 'scary looking' firearms illegal.

We all __need__ to work together to insure that the
"assault weapon" ban does not happen again, ever.

Ballistic Fingerprinting

The concept of "ballistic fingerprinting" is to have a spent casing on file by the authorities for every firearm. The theory is that every firearm creates unique markings on the case that can later be used to match them to the firearms that fired them.

Unfortunately, the entire premise is flawed, which eliminates any potential benefit. To begin with, the term "ballistic fingerprinting" is a misnomer. It implies that like human fingerprints, the markings created on fired cases do not change. Nothing could be further from the truth. Not only do the marks change slightly every time the gun is fired (by natural wear of metal against metal), but the parts that create the markings can also be easily altered with files or sandpaper or simply replaced.[42] The same gun will produce different markings on bullets and casings, and completely different guns can produce similar markings.[43] Criminals figured out the concept of filing off serial numbers over half a century ago. How long do you think it will take them to figure out how to change the "fingerprint"?

The gun grabbers, seeking to look like the good guys, state that the fingerprint database will allow police to trace guns. Let's assume for a minute that that is true. Considering that the overwhelming number of guns used in crimes are stolen,[44] the "fingerprints" will, at best, merely lead the police to the victim from whom gun was stolen. In New York and Maryland, where the ballistic database has been installed for several years, not a single prosecution based on matched casings for bullets has been reported.[45][46]

.50 Caliber Rifles

Bills have been introduced in Congress to ban the ownership and use of .50 caliber rifles by law-abiding citizens, because they are supposedly powerful enough that terrorists can use them to shoot down airplanes a mile away. While it sounds plausible and ominous to the average person, it could not be any more absurd. Even a highly trained and skilled marksman with perfect weather and no wind, cannot reliably hit a motionless target one mile away. Do you really think its possible to hit a target a mile away that is moving at 500 mph? And how is a single half-inch hole, placed at random, supposed to knock down a huge jet anyway? These rifles couldn't shoot down a biplane from World War I without a miraculously lucky hit. If today's airliners were really that fragile, no one would fly in them.

When that argument fails, the gun grabbers postulate that these rifles are used heavily by criminals. In reality, .50 caliber rifles have been used in only 18 crimes in the history of the United States. [47] I highly doubt that a gun that weighs 20 pounds, costs upwards of $6,000.00 each, and is four feet long, would be the gun of choice for a typical criminal.

Myth: Thirteen Children are Killed Each Day by Guns

This widely-quoted gun grabber statistic actually includes "children" as old as age 19 to 24, depending on the study. We know that most violent crime is perpetrated by males, ages 16-24. So, the numbers include adult gang members, and other criminals dying during the commission of crimes.[48] When criminals and suicides are removed, the actual number of "children" reduces to 1.3 [49]. While every death is a tragedy, the benefit of 2.5 million crimes stopped by citizens each year far outweighs the drawbacks.

Children and Guns

The gun grabbers would have you believe that children injured by guns is an epidemic in this country. They forget to inform the public that deaths involving firearms account for only 2% of all injuries to children age 0-14 years. Falls account for 3%, suffocation of ingesting an object is 4%, drowning 17%, and automobiles a whopping 51%[50]. With drownings eight times more likely to kill a child, why don't we see a group called "Women against Water"? Perhaps the greater good of water outweighs the risks?

Gun Registration

The case promoting gun registration is that it will help police solve crimes. History shows that the opposite is true. Common sense tells us that criminals won't register guns, so only the people who do not commit crimes will register. Even if a stolen gun is recovered during a criminal investigation, the gun will only be traced to the rightful owner, not the criminal. Hawaii, Chicago, and Washington D.C. (where registration is required) have not had even a single case where the laws have been instrumental in identifying someone who has committed a crime.[51]

Gun owners should rightly fear registration, as it is the first step to confiscation. Although denied by the gun grabbers, citizens in New York City, California, Canada, Germany, Australia, Bermuda, Cuba, Greece, Ireland, Jamaica, New Zealand, and Soviet Georgia are proof that registration leads to confiscation. Guns can be confiscated only if a registration list of their owners exist. Confiscation is the first step to genocide as witnessed by Nazi Germany and several other countries where millions have perrished.

Licensing

Licensing does nothing to stop crime. Criminals don't care about licenses. Even more absurd than that, the U.S. Supreme Court has ruled that *criminals* do not have to obtain licenses or register their weapons, as that would be an act of self-incrimination[52]. That leaves only law-abiding citizens to register, creating just another mechanism of registration and confiscation.

Automobiles are registered as a source of tax revenue. There are 228 million guns and only 207 million cars in this country, yet you are 31 times more likely to be accidentally killed by a car than a gun, according to the National Safety Council[53] — despite cars having been registered, and drivers licensed for almost 100 years.

Lawsuits

There has been a rash of city and state sponsored lawsuits attempting to penalize gun manufactures for the criminal use of their legally-made products. This is akin to blaming car manufacturers for drunk driving.

Mandatory Storage Laws

Fifteen states that passed "safe storage" laws for firearms saw 300 more murders, 3,860 more rapes, 24,650 more robberies, and over 25,000 more aggravated assaults in the first 5 years.[54] This is because a locked firearm is useless for defense. There is no decrease in either juvenile accidental gun deaths or suicides when such laws are enacted, but you do see an increase in crime.

Gun Show Loophole

Gun grabbers try to create pandemonium by proclaiming that criminals and terrorists have free access to guns by exploiting the "gun show loophole." The fact of the matter is that there is no such thing as a "gun show loophole." Gun dealers are federally licensed, and must follow the same rules for sales whether they are dealing from a storefront, or a gun show.[55]

The facts show that only 0.7% of convicts bought their firearms at gun shows,[56] while 93% of guns used in crimes are obtained illegally[57] (not from stores or gun shows).

Gun grabbers like to prove their case by stating that 25% of the vendors at most gun shows are "unlicensed dealers". True, but highly deceptive. About 25% of the booths at gun shows are occupied by dealers that do not sell guns, but feature knives, curios, accessories, books, etc. They do not deal in firearms, and do not *need* to be licensed.

Myth: Concealed Carry Laws Increase Crime

As of 2004, 36 states have right-to-carry laws. The majority of the American population lives in right-to-carry states, and in each, the crime rate fell after the right-to-carry law became active.

After passing their concealed carry law, Florida's homicide rate fell from 36% above the national average to 4% *below* the national average, and remains below the national average to this day.[58]

The serious crime rate in Texas fell 50% faster then the national average after a concealed carry law passed in 1995.

Crime is significantly higher in states without right-to-carry laws.[59]

Waiting Periods

The Federal "Brady Bill," and the laws of many states, require a citizen to wait as many as eight days or more to take possession of a gun after purchase. But no such nicety exists to delay criminals from perpetrating illegal activity.

Waiting periods threaten the safety of people in imminent danger:

- Bonnie Elmasri inquired about getting a gun to protect herself from a husband who had repeatedly threatened to kill her. She was told there was a 48-hour waiting period to buy a handgun. But unfortunately, Bonnie was never able to pick up a gun. She and her two sons were killed the next day by her abusive husband.[60]

- Marine Cpl. Rayna Ross bought a gun (in a non-waiting-period state) and used it to kill an attacker in self-defense two days later.[61] Had a 5-day waiting period been in effect, Ms. Ross would have been defenseless against the man who was stalking her.

- USA Today reported that many of the people rushing to gun stores during the 1992 riots were "lifelong gun control advocates, running to buy an item they thought they'd never need." Ironically, they were outraged to discover they had to wait 15 days to buy a gun for self-defense.[62]

Second Amendment

> *A well regulated Militia, being necessary to the security*
> *of a free State, the right of the people*
> *to keep and bear Arms, shall not be infringed.*

While numerous volumes can be, and have been, filled with Second Amendment arguments, I will just mention a few that I find particularly amusing:

Because the word 'militia' is used in the Second Amendment, gun control advocates claim that it does not describe an individual right, but a collective right to form and maintain a militia, which they further claim defines the modern-day National Guard. How can a document, ratified in 1791, refer to the National Guard, when Congress did not create the Guard until over 120 years later in 1913? Further evidence that the National Guard is not the same as the State Militias that previously existed can be found in the laws of many states. When the federal government took over the organized militias as part of the national military structure, many states, recognizing the potential need for such an organization under the sole control of the state, simply recreated the state militia system under another name. Today, many states have provision for such a "State Guard" force, and since 9/11, several of these units have a permanent identity, including active training.

How is it that all of the other amendments in the Bill of Rights bestow individual rights, yet the *second* amendment does not?

Walter Cronkite, holding a flintlock, purportedly stated that "this (flintlock) is what our founding fathers had in mind when they wrote the second amendment." If that is the case and our rights are restricted to flintlocks, the quill pen is what they had in mind when they wrote the first amendment and therefore, by using the same argument, the Constitution does not protect free speech on the Internet, television, radio, and in modern print media. It's funny that free speech, protected in the First Amendment, is so often used to vilify another constitutionally protected right.

This chapter is just the tip of the gun control iceberg. It behooves all gun owners to be familiar with the issues and lies surrounding our rights. Be aware of proposed legislation, on both the local and federal level, and fight to maintain your rights. After all, self-defense is a *human* right.

I want to acknowledge and sincerely thank Guy Smith, Alameda California, for his wonderful publication, "Gun Facts". His fantastic effort is the basis for most of the gun facts and gun control statistics cited in this book and should be read by every American. "Gun Facts" can be downloaded for free at: www.GunFacts.info.

RESOURCES

5.11 Tactical Series
761 Kearney Ave.
Modesto, CA 95350
(866) 451-1726
www.5.11tactical.com

Firearm Training Systems
7340 McGinnis Ferry Road
Suwanee, Georgia 30024
(800) 813-9046
www.fatsinc.com

Blade-Tech
2506 104th Street Court So.
Suite A
Lakewood, WA 98499
(253) 581-4347
www.blade-tech.com

Fist, Inc.
35 York Streer
Brooklyn, NY 11201
(800) 443-3478
www.fistholsters.com

Coronado Leather Company
1059 Tierra Del Rey, Suite C
Chula Vista, CA 91910
(800) 283-9509
www.coronadoleather.com

Galco International
2019 West Quail Avenue
Phoenix, Arizona 85027
(800) USGALCO
www.usgalco.com

Crimson Trace
8089 SW Cirrus Drive
Beaverton OR 97008
(800) 442-2406
www.crimsontrace.com

IDPA - International
Defensive Pistol Association
2232 CR 719
Berryville, AR 72616
(870) 545-3886
www.idpa.com

Defense Security Products
3-01 Park Plaza, Suite 108
Old Brookville
New York 11545
(800) 830-3057
www.thunderwear.com

Insight Technology Inc.
3 Technology Drive
Londonderry, NH 03053
(877) 744-4802
www.insightlights.com

IPSC - International Practical Shooting Confederation
PO Box 972 Oakville
Ontario Canada L6J 9Z9
(905) 849-6960
www.ipsc.org

Kramer Handgun Leather
P.O. Box 112154
Tacoma, WA 98411
(800) 510-2666
www.kramerleather.com

LaserMax, Inc.
3495 Winton Place,
Rochester, NY 14623
(585) 272-5427
www.lasermax-inc.com

Les Baer Custom
29601 34th Ave.
Hillsdale, IL 61257
(309) 658-2716
www.lesbaer.com

Mitch Rosen Extraordinary Gunleather
300 Bedford Street
Manchester, NH 03101
(603) 647-2971
www.mitchrosen.com

Novack's LLC
2 Klarides Village Drive
Suite 336
Seymour, CT 06483
(203) 262-6484
www.precisionsights.com

Pager Pal
200 W. Pleasantview
Hurst, TX. 76054
(800) 561-1603
www.pagerpal.com

Pelican Products, Inc.
23215 Early Avenue,
Torrance, CA 90505
(800) 473-5422
www.pelican.com/lights.html

Rifle Locker
Phoenix USA
(800) 894-4858
www.gunlocker.com

**Ruger
Sturm, Ruger & Co., Inc.**
Lacey Place
Southport, CT 06890
(203) 259-7843
www.ruger-firearms.com

Sigarms, Inc.
18 Industrial Drive
Exeter, NH 03833
(603) 772-2302
www.sigarms.com

Simunition
65 Sandscreen Road
Avon, CT, 06001
(860) 404-0162
www.simunition.com

Smith & Wesson
2100 Roosevelt Avenue
Springfield, MA 01104
(800) 331-0852
www.smith-wesson.com

Springfield Armory
420 West Main Street
Geneseo, Illinois 61254
(800) 680-6866
www.springfield-armory.com

Streamlight, Inc.
30 Eagleville Road,
Eagleville, PA. 19403
(800) 523-7488
www.streamlight.com

SureFire, LLC
18300 Mount Baldy Circle
Fountain Valley, CA 92708
(800) 828-8809
www.surefire.com

Taurus
16175 NW 49 Ave.
Miami, FL 33014
(305) 624-1115
www.taurususa.com

Thunderwear
Defense Security Products
3-01 Park Plaza, Suite 108
Old Brookville, NY 11545
(800) 830-3057
www.thunderwear.com

Trijicon, Inc.
49385 shafer Avenue
Wixom, MI 48393
(800) 338-0563
www. trijicon.com

Truglo, Inc.
13745 Neutron Rd.
Dallas, TX 75244
(972) 774-0300
www.truglosights.com

USPSA - United States
Practical Shooting Assoc.
P.O. Box 811
Sedro-Woolley, WA 98284
(360) 855-2245
www.uspsa.com

Winchester Ammunition
427 North Shamrock Street
East Alton, IL 62024
(618) 258-2000
www.winchester.com

XS Sight Systems
2401 Ludelle
Fort Worth, Texas 76105
(888) 744-4880
www.expresssights.com

ENDNOTES

[1] Dial 911 and Die. Richard W. Stevens. Mazel Freedom Press. P.12

[2] DeShaney V. Winnebago County Dep't. of Soc. Servs,. 489 U.S. 189 109S Ct. 998, 103 L. Ed. 2d 249 (1989)

[3] Id., 489 U.S. at 195 (internal citations and parenthetical explanations omitted here for brevity).

[4] "The Law of Self-defense: A Guide for the Armed Citizen". Andrew F. Branca. Operion Security. Pg. 92

[5] "Warren on Homicide" Oscar L. Warren. Hein & Company, Inc. 1914

[6] Black Belt magazine, Ralph Mroz. Volume 41, No. 8, August 2003. Black Belt Communications, Inc. Pgs. 80-81.

[7] "How Close is Too Close?", SWAT magazine. March 1983.

[8] "Providence Journal", December 28, 2001

[9] Defensive Shooting for Real-Life Encounters, Ralph Mroz. Paladin Press. Pgs. 130-131

[10] Sigarms, Inc. 18 Industrial Drive, Exeter, NH 03833 (603)772-2302 www.sigarms.com

[11] Novack's LLC 2 Klarides Village Drive, Suite 336, Seymour, CT 06483 (203)262-6484 www.precisionsights.com

[12] LaserMax, Inc. 3495 Winton Place, Rochester, NY 14623 (585)-272-5427 www.lasermax-inc.com

[13] Crimson Trace Lasers 8089 SW Cirrus Drive, Beaverton OR 97008 (800)442-2406) (503)627-9992 www.crimsontrace.com

[14] "A Rifleman Went to War". Herbert W. McBride. Lancer Militaria, 1987 (reprint), p. 178

[15] Coronado Leather Company 1059 Tierra Del Rey, Suite C Chula Vista, CA 91910 800-283-9509 www.coronadoleather.com

[16] 5.11 Tactical Series 761 Kearney Ave. Modesto, CA 95350 866-451-1726 www.5.11tactical.com

[17] Galco International 2019 West Quail Avenue, Phoenix, Arizona 85027 (800) USGALCO www.usgalco.com

[18] Defense Security Products 3-01 Park Plaza, Suite 108 Old Brookville, New York 11545 (800)830-3057 www.thunderwear.com

[19] Pager Pal 200 W. Pleasantview, Hurst, TX. 76054 (800)561-1603 www.pagerpal.com

[20] Kramer Handgun Leather P.O. Box 112154 Tacoma, WA 98411 (800) 510-2666 www.kramerleather.com

[21] Fist, Inc. 35 York St., Brooklyn, NY 11201 (800) 443-3478 www.fistholsters.com

[22] Mitch Rosen Extraordinary Gunleather, LLC 300 Bedford Street, Manchester, NH 03101 (603) 647-2971 www.mitchrosen.com

[23] Simunition 65 Sandscreen Road, Avon, CT, 06001 USA 860-404-0162 www.simunition.com

[24] www.idpa.com

[26] www.ipsc.org & www.uspsa.org

[26] SureFire, LLC   18300 Mount Baldy Circle Fountain Valley, CA 92708 800-828-8809 www.surefire.com

[27] Streamlight, Inc. 30 Eagleville Road, Eagleville, PA. 19403 800-523-7488 www.streamlight.com

[28] Pelican Products, Inc. 23215 Early Avenue, Torrance, CA 90505 800-473-5422 www.pelican.com/lights.html

[29] "CNN rapped over gun segment". Robert Stacy McCain. www.washtimes.com/national/20030519-110144-7123r.htm

[30] "Under the Gun: Weapons Crime, and Violence in America". Bureau of Alcohol, Tobacco and Firearms estimate and reported via James Wright, Peter H. Rossi, Kathleen Daly. 1983

[31] "More Guns Less Crime". John R. Lott. The University of Chicago Press, 1998

[32] Dr. Gary Kleck, University of Florida using FBI Uniform Crime Statistics, 1997

[33] "Index of Crime by State". FBI Uniform Crime Reports for 2000, p. 79, Table 5,

[34] Ibid

[35] "More Guns Less Crime". John R. Lott. The University of Chicago Press, 1998

[36] U.S. Department of Justice, Law Enforcement Assistance Administration, Rape Victimization in 26 American Cities, 1979, p. 31.

[37] "The Armed Criminal in America: A Survey of Incarcerated Felons," U.S. Department of Justice, National Institute of Justice. Research Report, July 1985. P 27.

[38] "Point Blank. Guns and Violence in America". Gary Kleck, 1991. PP. 111-116, 148.

[39] "Are We a Nation of Cowards'?," George F. Will. Newsweek. November 15, 1993. P. 93

[40] Violence Policdy Center http://www.vpc.org/studies/awaconc.htm

[41] "Targeting Guns". Gary Keck. 1997, compilation of 48 metropolitan police departments from 1980-1994

[42] "Feasibility of a Ballistics Imaging Database for All New Handgun Sales", Frederick Tulleners,. California Dept. of Justice, Bureau of Forensic Services, October, 2001

[43] "Handbook of Firearms & Ballistics: Examining and Interpreting Forensic Evidence", Heard, 1997

[44] "Armed and Considered Dangerous", U.S. Department of Justice, 1986

[45] "Ballistics 'fingerprinting' not foolproof". Baltimore Sun, October 15, 2002

[46] "Townsend backs New Rule on Sale of Assault Rifles". Washington Post, October 30, 2002

[47] "Weaponry: .50 Caliber Rifle Crime". General Accounting Office, Report no. OSI-99-15R, Revised Oct. 21, 2001

[48] FBI Uniform Crime Statistics, 1997

[49] Validated using Center for Disease Control, National Vital Statistics Report – Deaths: Final Data for 1998, July 24, 2000, Table 8, Page 26

[50] "Injury Facts". National Safety Council. 1999 — figures rounded for ease of display

[51], "Gun Licensing Leads to Increased Crime, Lost Lives". Prof. John Lott. L.A. Times, Aug. 23, 2000

[52] Hayes vs. U.S. 390 U.S. 85 1968

[53] Automobile estimate: Federal Highway Administration, October 1998. Firearm estimate: FBI Uniform Crime Statistics, 1996

[54] "Safe Storage Gun Laws: Accidental Deaths, Suicides, and Crime". Prof. John Lott. Yale School of Law, March 2000

[54] Bureau of Alcohol, Tobacco, and Firearms, June 2000, covers only July 1996 through December 1998

[55] "Firearm Use by Offenders". Bureau of Justice Statistics, November 2001

[57] Bureau of Alcohol, Tobacco, and Firearms, 1999

[58] "Shall issue: the new wave of concealed handgun permit laws". C. Cramer and D. Kopel. Golden CO: Independence Instate Issue Paper. October 17, 1994

[59] John Lott, David Mustard: This study involved county level crime statistics from all 3,054 counties in the U.S. from 1977 through 1992

[60] Congressional Record, May 8, 1991. pp. H 2859, H 2862

[61] Wall Street Journal, March 1994. P. A10

[62] "Survival for the armed," Jonathan T. Lovitt. USA Today. May 4, 1992